ANCIENT EGYPT

ON 5 DEBEN A DAY

Everywhere they travel, visitors to Egypt will find monumental testaments to Egypt's wealth and might, such as this pylon at Karnak Temple.

DONALD P. RYAN

ANCIENT EGYPT
ON 5 DEBEN A DAY

with 88 illustrations, 12 in color

CONTENTS

I · MAKING THE JOURNEY

Understanding the Egyptians • When To Go
Money Matters • Getting There • Things To Bring With You
Accommodation and Other Issues

So you're thinking about visiting Egypt? You may have heard the rumours: the culture is confounding, the language is perplexing, the local people are suspicious of foreigners, there are no tourist facilities and an aggressive, egocentric pharaoh rules the land. All these things are true. The Egyptians see themselves as the centre of the universe and consider their ruler to be a living god on earth.

On the other hand, you may have heard tales of a rich and verdant land of unsurpassed achievements in the arts and engineering, and great monuments to its gods and divine rulers. These things are likewise true. Egypt is a veritable breadbasket, with the waters of the great Nile river feeding endless green fields, providing food for its people and habitat for an abundance of fish and fowl. Egypt's distinct civilization has already survived for at least two millennia, giving it plenty of time for its culture to develop. Its incredible temples and funerary monuments will astonish even the most jaded traveller. Nothing in Mesopotamia, Crete or Mycenae can even compete in terms of sheer grandeur. Indeed, most of the Egyptian people – at least the ones with tolerable jobs – love life so much that they wish to continue it in the next world, for instance, by preserving the body after death.

Egypt is indeed truly spectacular. Its many wonders will reward well the bold and adventurous time-traveller. Right now, well into the reign of Ramesses II, Egypt is prosperous, energetic and full of ambition, and more hospitable to foreigners than ever before (which admittedly isn't saying much!). It's a great time to visit.

UNDERSTANDING THE EGYPTIANS

To a foreign visitor, Egyptian attitudes towards outsiders may appear a bit chilly, if not downright xenophobic, and a little understanding on your part will go a long way. The Egyptians see themselves as the chief beneficiaries of the gods, who have provided them with a splendid land that they call Kemet, literally 'the black land', referring to the dark alluvial soil created by the annual flooding of the Nile, which has provided the rich agrarian foundation for their civilization. Another name for Egypt is 'Ta-mery': 'the beloved land'. The Egyptians indeed love their land and feel passionately connected to it. To be an Egyptian is to strive to live in harmony with the land and the forces of the universe. Those who are not Egyptian – you, for instance – historically were perceived as potential agents of chaos who might disrupt the stable cosmic order and trigger calamity. So if you're interrogated for hours at the border and the guard won't look you in the eye, don't take it personally; he's doing his civic duty to protect Egypt from fire, hail and locusts.

This distrust of foreigners is also understandable in light of a traumatic military invasion Egypt recently endured. For many centuries, the Egyptians had lived a fairly spoiled existence; vast and intimidating deserts to the west and east, a series of rapids in the Nile to the south, and the immense Mediterranean sea to the north protected them from any serious external threats. Then, just a few hundred years ago, the Hyksos, a group of people native to the east, were able to wrest control over the land, and for the first time in its history, part of Egypt was ruled by foreigners. This, of course, was utterly intolerable to the Egyptians and after 100 years of humiliation, they were able to drive out the invaders. Not long afterwards, the Egyptians began an aggressive campaign of empire-building, especially to the east, even using new technology adopted from the Hyksos, such as the chariot and the curved sword, to their own advantage.

Because of these recent campaigns of conquest, many people living in the lands of the eastern Mediterranean have

---

A POPULAR STORY

A popular story in Egypt involves an Egyptian bureaucrat named Sinuhe who flees in fear from his beloved homeland after the death of the pharaoh he served. He establishes himself in a foreign land where he becomes quite successful, yet he longs passionately for Kemet, desiring to return there to die in his old age. The happy ending has Sinuhe returning home to great welcome and reverting to his native culture.

---

probably already met some Egyptians. The warrior-pharaohs of the last couple of hundred years have brought their armies barrelling east through Canaan and beyond, attacking cities along the way, demanding tribute for the homeland, and establishing armed garrisons to maintain compliance and order. Egypt has become incredibly rich as a result of its empire-building, and you'll see evidence of this newfound wealth in Ramesses' lavish monuments, palaces and public works when you visit.

As a non-Egyptian, accept that you will be considered an outsider. But this doesn't mean that you will be alone: despite its traditional distrust of foreigners, in the time of Ramesses II, Egypt actually hosts many people from abroad. There are mercenaries from Nubia and elsewhere, and prisoners of war from far and wide employed in a variety of

Some people enter Egypt against their will – these bound foreign captives, for instance.

government and religious institutions, though usually in servile positions. Merchants and emissaries from distant lands are coming and going, some doing business, others bearing messages or paying tribute and homage to Egypt's ruler. Here and there you will actually find colonies of cooperative foreigners, including refugees from famines outside Egypt. Several Egyptian rulers have even had foreign wives or hosted foreigners in their households, either as peace hostages or to strengthen diplomatic alliances. (Ramesses II himself has two Hittite wives and several Syrian butlers.)

With all this in mind, it is indeed possible for a foreigner to visit Egypt, but the less you draw attention to yourself as an outsider, the better your experience is likely to be. Do your best to conform to the order and flow of Egyptian society while maintaining a respectful attitude

THE EGYPTIANS

The Egyptians tend to classify people as one of four kinds: Egyptians, Libyans to the West, Nubians to the South and Asiatics to the North or East. If you don't match any of these categories, the Egyptians will likely find a way to fit you into one or another.

RIGHT: *Libyan, Nubian or Asiatic: how will the Egyptians categorize you?*

towards any odd customs you may encounter. While you can't necessarily expect to be welcomed everywhere with open arms, your cultural sensitivity will likely impress your Egyptian hosts.

WHEN TO GO

CHOOSING THE APPROPRIATE time to visit Egypt is essential. The Egyptians themselves divide their year into three seasons composed of four months, each linked to their annual agricultural schedule. Akhet (roughly mid-July–mid-November) is the time of the annual flooding, or 'inundation', of the Nile river. Peret (mid-November–mid-March) is the period of crop growing, and Shemu (mid-March–mid-July) is harvest time.

All things considered, the best overall time for a visit to Egypt is Peret into early Shemu (although if you're arriving by sea, there are other factors to consider; see p. 11). The extent of the inundation can vary from year to year and limits some forms of travel during Akhet. It can be a bit hot for much of the early season and the latter part of Shemu. Peret is probably the optimal time to travel within Egypt. The climate should be lovely and the fields lush and green.

BELOW: *As a foreigner visiting Egypt, don't expect a warm welcome at the border.*

DURING YOUR TOUR

During your tour through Egypt, you'll notice numerous conical beehive-shaped structures punctuating the landscape. These are the silos that store Egypt's bounty of grain. Constructed of mud-brick in various sizes, they stand ready to pay out the wages of workmen and serve as food reserves in case of famine.

in the values and costs of various items, and practise your haggling skills at every possible opportunity en route. Flexibility is essential, as prices may vary from one place to another, but be on the lookout for the occasional dishonest trader who might try to exploit your ignorance as an outsider. Traditional Egyptian wisdom has much to say about honest dealings in commerce, so if you see a thumb on the scale or think you've been offered a sack of rocks in lieu of barley, you might quote the following passage from

MONEY MATTERS

ANOTHER IMPORTANT consideration in travelling to Egypt is the matter of payment for goods and services. The Egyptians operate on a kind of barter economy. The value of various items is based on a comparison to standard units, the most common being called a 'deben' which is actually equivalent to .91 grams of copper. One deben, for example, is equivalent to a sack of emmer wheat. As Egypt is an intensely agricultural land, it perhaps makes sense that set quantities of grain and beer, the staples of the realm, are the standard payments made to workers. The average worker's daily wage consists of ten loaves of bread and up to two jars of beer. These commodities can be exchanged for other food items, clothing or tools, which can be swapped for other desirable things in turn.

To make the barter system work for you, you'll need to become well versed

COMMODITY PRICES

Here is a sample of a few current commodity prices:

◆ ◆ ◆

1 sack or basketful of barley	1–2 deben
1 donkey	25–40 deben, depending on quality
1 cow	50 deben
1 duck	½ deben
1 large container of beer (25 litres)	1–2 deben
1 jar of wine	2 deben
1 jar of sesame oil	1 deben
1 bundle of vegetables	½ deben
1 tunic	4–5 deben
1 skirt	15 deben

the teachings of the sage Amenemope, which exhort the merchant:

Do not move the scales nor alter the weights,
Nor diminish the fractions of the measure...
Beware of disguising the measure,
So as to falsify its fractions.

This, of course, is an ideal and such wisdom only comes from first-hand experience of abuse. Don't let it discourage you from learning to barter like a native.

MONEY

Money in the form of coins won't appear until over 500 years after the reign of Ramesses II. These early coins will be created from electrum and minted in the kingdom of Lydia in Anatolia (modern-day Turkey). The idea will quickly become popular and spread to Egypt when the Greeks gain control after an invasion by Alexander the Great.

As a visitor to Egypt, you won't be receiving your daily worker's ration of bread and beer to use as money. You might do well, therefore, to enter the land with a quantity of silver or gold that can than be converted into more fluid commodities. While a deben of copper is the standard unit of exchange, other precious metals such as silver and gold can also be used. Silver in particular is highly valued, with a deben of silver possessing a value sixty times greater than that of copper. Its high value to weight makes it a far more practical option for travellers than bulkier commodities. Carry it discreetly (for example, as bracelets on your arms and ankles, hidden by clothing) and go your humble way, doing your best not to clank and jingle too audibly.

GETTING THERE

To GET TO EGYPT, YOU HAVE two basic travel options: by land or by sea, both with their advantages and disadvantages. If you are starting your journey almost anywhere on the perimeter of the Mediterranean, Egypt is easily accessible by ship, as foreign boats regularly deliver a variety of desirable items to the Black Land. Egyptian boats, too, are active in the Mediterranean but much scarcer north of places such as Byblos on the Levantine coast. Although the Egyptians masterfully use the Nile river as a domestic highway, they are not great seafarers in open waters and tend to be shore-huggers. Despite this handicap, Egyptian ships still manage to travel great distances: Egyptian navigators have, on occasion, followed the Red Sea coast all the way down to the land of Punt on the horn of Africa to bring back magnificent exotic goods, including living trees and wild animals.

The Egypt of Ramesses II is a booming commercial enterprise. At the ports, you'll see wine, wood and other exotic goods being unloaded.

Travelling direct by boat will certainly get you to Egypt more quickly than walking (or riding a donkey) via the land route – provided that your ship doesn't encounter marauders or stop repeatedly to do business at various ports. It's also important to consider the season, as the most favourable conditions for navigation on the Mediterranean are from the end of May until mid-September. Very experienced sailors might venture out in the transitional seasons of spring and autumn, but winter should be avoided at all costs due to the unpredictable storms that can easily sink the average merchant ship.

In any event, if you choose the maritime route to Egypt, your first order of business is to select a suitable port of departure and get on board a ship. Some of the busiest ports, such as Byblos, Sidon and Tyre, can be found in Phoeni-cian coastal territory. Further south, you might try your luck on the Canaan coast: Dor, Ashdod and Ashkelon are relatively close to Egypt. If coming from the northern or north-eastern Mediter-ranean, ports abound, although politi-cal conflicts brewing in the Aegean might prove disruptive.

As tourist travel to Egypt is the excep-tion rather than the norm, you'll have to find some way to convince the ship's captain or its owner that it is worthwhile to take you on board. This will more than likely involve an exchange of items or labour, or perhaps a bribe. However you bargain, expect to bring your own food and sleep on the deck or perhaps in an uncomfortable spot in the cargo hold. In some cases, you might very well be asked to help out with the ship's chores and your ability to row might be considered an advantage. However, ask around about the reputation of your ship beforehand, as you certainly want to avoid the possibility of being asked to row for a good long time...as a slave!

Assuming all goes well and you avoid shipwreck or enslavement, you'll approach the land of Egypt from its Mediterranean coast. The captain will then journey south through one of the Nile's several branches that transect the river's delta region, an area that the Egyptians call 'Lower Egypt'. At the first major port on the Nile, the captain, his crew and accompanying goods will likely be examined. (Should you be questioned, refer to the instructions below regarding entering Egypt by land.) Once in Egypt, you might carry on south with the boat that brought

you, or beg or buy a ride on the many domestic boats you'll find coming and going.

If, on the other hand, you decide to enter Egypt by land, the easiest and most heavily travelled route follows the coast south through the land of Canaan until eventually reaching Gaza, which essentially serves as a satellite Egyptian bureaucratic centre. From there, a well-trodden path of about 150 miles will bring you to Egypt's eastern border. The Egyptians refer to this route as 'the Ways of Horus', an interesting name with ominous overtones: it is the path that the pharaohs, considered living embodiments of the god Horus, have repeatedly used in their conquest and subjugation of territories to the east.

Military forts in frontier territories protect Egyptian travellers and intimidate the neighbours.

AN EGYPTIAN TALE

A popular Egyptian tale involves a travelling peasant whose goods are confiscated by an abusive landowner. When his situation is brought before the authorities, the unfortunate visitor is asked to plead his case repeatedly because of his superb speaking skills. His words so impress the pharaoh that he orders justice to be done, and the substantial property of the abuser is awarded to 'the eloquent peasant'.

Blame those pesky Hyksos, if you like, but the fact remains that the Egyptians are actively guarding their homeland far from their capital. The Ways of Horus is punctuated by military outposts and forts approximately every 10–12 miles, a reasonable day's travel for an army regiment. While the constant presence of Egyptian military garrisons might feel intimidating, remember that they do help keep the peace and ultimately make your journey a bit safer.

Plan on taking about ten days to two weeks to travel the Ways of Horus, depending on how fast you're trekking. There are wells or reservoirs for water at the military outposts and these establishments are relatively well supplied to support their guardians. At the western end of the road is the eastern frontier of Egypt, announced by the impressive fort of Tjaru, where you pass through a gate and cross a bridge spanning a crocodile-infested canal. Pay no attention to the crocodiles; pass through another gate and proceed to the interview.

Don't be too intimidated by the border guards; the Egyptians just want to make sure you know who's in charge from the very beginning. Given that you will probably be asked to 'state your business', some practical advice is in order:

The Egyptian guardians will want to know the purpose of your visit to Egypt. Just stating that you 'want to have a look around' is not good enough. Any kind of reasonable commercial or diplomatic business is preferred and if you can convince them that you have relatives in Egypt, or some personal connection with an Egyptian (the more highly placed the better), your chances of passing are greatly improved.

Appear non-threatening. If you've been travelling with weapons, get rid of them, especially if you are in a group. A passive, if not dramatically submissive, demeanour will help to produce the desirable outcome.

Let the most eloquent member of your group do the speaking. The Egyptians admire good speech. A few comments about the beauty of Egypt's landscape, the sophistication of its culture and the greatness, majesty and benevolence of Ramesses II will go a long way.

The other routes into Egypt are riskier and not recommended for tourists.

There are maritime routes into the Nile Valley from the Red Sea, but ships are not particularly frequent and there are dangerous shoals and reefs to contend with, followed by an arduous overland traverse westward that will take you days to reach the Nile Valley. There is also a land route that some of the nomadic tribes use for coming into Egypt from the Sinai. This route is likewise not recommended unless you are an experienced desert traveller or, better yet, a member of the aforementioned nomadic tribes. It is possible to enter Egypt from the south, via Nubia, but this journey is also not easy and you will have to run the gauntlet of numerous protective forts south of the border. It's probably best to stick with either a Mediterranean ship or the Ways of Horus route from Canaan.

THINGS TO BRING
WITH YOU

ITEMS FOR BARTER Specialty or artisan items from your homeland will fetch a good price; the Egyptians are very fond of exotic goods. Little trinkets are also useful as tokens of appreciation for hospitality, or for the occasional bribe.

BEAST(S) OF BURDEN If you are travelling by land, you will probably want to procure a sturdy donkey or two for carrying your items. With luck, your donkey-dealer will help you select a cooperative beast; an ancient or sick donkey might not survive the journey and one that bites, spins or continually brays will make your life a misery. Donkeys can also be traded as commodities in an emergency, or sold if no longer required when you enter or leave Egypt.

SANDALS If you're on foot, you might wear through a few pairs, so bring some extras if you want to wear your favourite brand. Footwear, however, is readily available in Egypt, including lightweight styles manufactured from the papyrus plant.

A STOUT STICK A walking stick is a very useful travelling tool. It can also be used to swat your uncooperative donkey, shoo away approaching

A sturdy braying donkey can carry all of your belongings, and then some.

snarling dogs and small children, or as an impromptu weapon to use against highway robbers. An added bonus is that staffs are a sign of authority in Egypt; carrying a stick will create the impression that you are a foreigner of some import!

CLOTHES You will want to carry a few changes of clothes, unless you are trying to enter the country under the pretence of being some sort of economic refugee. In general, the Egyptians will not be receptive to a visiting foreigner who smells bad and dresses in a slovenly manner. (To refine your understanding of Egyptian sartorial standards, see Chapter II.) If you are coming by land or sea during the winter, clothes made of wool will offer better protection from the cold and damp on your journey. Much lighter and comfortable clothes can be purchased on arrival in Egypt.

BLANKETS Bedroom accommodation in and en route to Egypt is not guaranteed. A collection of woollen blankets will keep you warm wherever you have to sleep, and can also be used as a makeshift shawl. Provided that they aren't in too shabby a condition, the blankets might also make good barter items, especially if they are decorative.

ACCOMMODATION AND OTHER ISSUES

DESPITE THE RISING NUMBER of foreigners in Egypt under Ramesses II, the Egyptian hospitality industry is still pretty meager; that is to say, practically nonexistent. Most foreign travellers are on official business (including those being towed behind the army as prisoners of war) and already have a place to go. As such, don't expect comfortable and well-appointed inns welcoming you on every corner. If coming by land, be prepared to camp along the route if no accommodation is available. A tent or some blankets next to a fire on the side of the road might be suitable. (And keep that stick handy!) Occasionally, occupants of the Egyptian garrisons might be persuaded to assist you in return for a small 'gift'. While in Egypt itself, expect much of the same unless you make friends in high places, who may have access to diplomatic or other official accommodation. As you meet friendly or cooperative Egyptians, ask them for recommendations as to where you might stay at your next destination. If all else fails, offer something of value to a friendly-looking villager and you might be rewarded with a bearable night's stay and an edible meal.

II · PRACTICAL CONSIDERATIONS

Food and Drink ✦ *Clothing* ✦ *Sanitation*
Medical Emergencies ✦ *The Rules* ✦ *Egyptian Religion*
Gods' Mansions and Gods' Servants ✦ *As We Progress...*

AS A TRAVELLER TO EGYPT, YOU no doubt have a number of questions regarding the bare necessities: What do I eat? What's the dress code? How can I avoid illness and what do I do in a health emergency? How do I stay out of trouble? Some insights into Egyptian religious practices will also prove invaluable. This chapter will address these topics to prepare you better for an Egyptian tourist experience.

FOOD AND DRINK

THE CHANCE THAT YOU WILL ever starve in Egypt is remote unless you're unlucky enough to arrive during a year of crop pestilence or low Nile floods. Even the poorest inhabitants of the land seem adequately fed. Egyptian culture promotes generosity and the sharing of food, and the natural benefits of the Nile, along with advanced irrigation and agricultural practices, have made Egypt a breadbasket.

The essential food staples of Egypt are bread and beer, which are made from emmer wheat and barley, the two main grain crops. Egyptian bread is produced in several dozen different varieties. At its simplest, it consists of flour, water and a little salt. Other kinds are delightfully sweet and flavoured with honey and dates. You will notice, too, that bread comes in many different shapes. The round flat loaves are the most common variety but others are made in triangular or even cone shapes. Flatbreads can be cooked in ovens or on a stone in a fire. Another baking method involves a tube-like ceramic oven. Bread dough is slapped on its walls and then peeled off when cooked. For some of the more interesting bread shapes such as cones, pottery moulds are used to contain the dough as it cooks in an oven. Anyway you have it, Egyptian bread is healthy

EGYPTIAN BREAD

Egyptian bread is delicious, but it can be hard on your teeth. You will notice that the teeth of the locals, especially the older ones, are typically worn or even chipped. This is because the process of threshing, winnowing and grinding grain leaves grit, sand and occasionally small fragments of gravel in the flour that end up in the bread and gradually file down the teeth.

and satisfying. Fresh and warm out of the oven, it is a genuine treat. You'll be eating lots of it.

The production of beer, the favourite beverage of the land, is closely related to that of bread. Partially baked barley bread crumbs are added to fresh water and allowed to ferment in a jar. When the desired alcohol content is reached, the beer is strained and transferred into beer jugs, ready for consumption. As workmen are typically paid in beer, it can't be terribly strong, lest it impede performance at the worksite. Beer is even given to school-age boys in their lunches. For those living away from the banks of the Nile, beer is probably a much tastier, more carbohydrate-rich and healthier alternative to village canal water. Tourists, too, should adopt beer as their preferred beverage – with any luck its alcohol content will help kill some of the more disagreeable creatures living in the local water. This is no hardship; Egyptian beer is delicious and available in various strengths, often enhanced with honey or other sweeteners.

While on the subject of alcoholic beverages, wine is available as a luxury item for special occasions. The best local wine tends to be produced in the Fayyum and Delta regions and from the oases in the western desert, and imports from foreign lands such as Canaan are also well appreciated. Grapes are nurtured in well-watered and tended vineyards and then processed by foot. The resulting juice is stored in jars where it naturally ferments. These jars are sealed and typically stamped or marked with their source. Apart from grapes, other fruits – including figs, dates and pomegranates – can likewise be used to produce sweet, delicious wines suitable for any celebration.

Locally produced Egyptian wine is expensive but wonderful for those special occasions.

Vegetables thrive in 'the Black Land' and are an important part of the Egyptian diet. Onions and garlic are plentiful, as are cucumbers and lettuce. Chickpeas, beans, lentils and a variety of peas are also grown. Porridges and vegetable stews with meat, fish and fowl are popular and the recipes are enlivened by condiments such as coriander and cumin. The typical Egyptian workman's lunch consists of some raw onions and cucumbers with bread, and a jug of beer to wash it down. This may often be your own lunch as you travel through Kemet.

Although you will probably see lots of cattle being herded down dusty roads or grazing in fields, most of these animals are kept for milk or used as plough animals. Beef is quite expensive and is rarely eaten by commoners; it is primarily a food of the wealthy. If your host serves you roast ox, you should feel very honoured indeed. More affordable meat comes from what the Egyptians refer to as 'small cattle': sheep, goats and sometimes pigs. Birds, including ducks and geese, are also readily available to the average worker and can be enjoyed roasted, grilled or made into stews. They are caught in nets and snares, or sometimes subdued with throwing sticks or arrows. Fish, too, are plentiful and on the banks of the Nile you can observe fishermen at work in skiffs made from bundles of naturally buoyant papyrus stalks, using scoop-, throw- and seine-nets along with fish traps and lines with hooks. There's nothing to beat freshly caught Nile perch baked in the ashes of

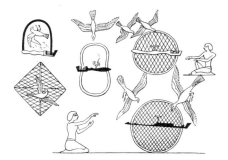

Trapping birds in nets can be hard work but ultimately delicious.

a fire. The rest of the catch can be preserved by drying or salting.

The Egyptians eat well and so should you. Should you be lucky enough to be invited to a celebratory banquet, especially an affair put on by the elite of Egyptian society, the food will be lavish and delicious, and as always, plenty of bread and beer will be available.

THE AFTERLIFE

What do the Egyptians desire in the afterlife? More of the same things they enjoyed in life, including their beloved staple foods. Symbolic offerings to the dead represent bread and beer, lots of it, as much as a thousand jugs and loaves depicted in a single tomb painting. Cattle and fowl are also popular meals for the spirits of the deceased.

CLOTHING

TRAVELLING AS A FOREIGNER, you'll want to decide whether to conform to local customs. Should you choose to present yourself as an outsider

The tubular sheath dress has long been popular with fashionable ladies.
What the best-dressed bureaucrats are wearing these days.

in your usual garb, make sure your clothes are clean and presentable, as the Egyptians perceive foreigners to be dirty and unkempt, much as they might be fascinated by your exotic attire.

On the other hand, it might be better to go native and dress in the manner of an Egyptian, preferably one of some importance. As everywhere, clothes reflect one's social status. At one extreme are manual labourers clad in filthy loincloths; at the other, royal family members and top bureaucrats in pleated, gleaming white outfits unsoiled by manual labour. It should be obvious which group it is best to imitate.

Men of status usually wear a wraparound skirt or kilt of linen secured at the waist and sometimes accompanied by an apron or a sash over the shoulder. The kilt can be worn with a tunic–shirt, but a knee- or ankle-length tunic, secured at the waist, can also serve as a fashionable garment. For the ladies, the tubular sheath dress has been popular for centuries. It is typically form-fitting and is

PRICE OF CLOTHING

Prices of clothing vary depending on the quality of the linen or other materials. You can expect to pay somewhere between 3 and 5 deben for a tunic and between 10 and 50 for a skirt. The lowly loincloth costs 5–16 deben and a shawl or cloak, 20–50. By comparison, sandals are quite a bargain and average around 2 deben per pair.

Elaborate hairstyles of the well-to-do. Don't be deceived: most are wigs!

held up by shoulder straps, either with or without the breasts exposed. The lovely dancing girls who perform at parties might wear a fishnet dress or nothing more than a belt with a few dangling bead tassels. Shawls and cloaks are worn by both men and women for fashion and warmth. Sandals manufactured from strips of papyrus or constructed from leather are available, although many workers prefer to go barefoot. The

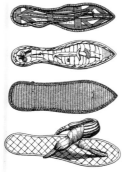

Some examples of fine Egyptian footwear.

children of Egypt typically scamper about quite naked; even their heads are shorn bare, save a sidelock of hair that signifies youth.

Egyptians of both sexes pay a good amount of attention to hair and make-up. Men's hairstyles, for example, range from the comfortable, closely cropped coiffures of the working man to the long elaborate wigs worn by members of the upper classes. Mirrors of polished bronze assist in the application of eye make-up, which is made from a dark-grey powdered pigment called *mesdemet* (kohl) and worn by both women and men from all walks of life. You might try some on yourself: *mesdemet* is thought to protect the eyes from both the bright sun and ocular diseases, which are not unusual in Egypt.

GOLD

As in most cultures around the Mediterranean, gold is highly prized in Egypt for its beautiful gleaming colour and amazing malleability. The Egyptians refer to this metal poetically as the 'flesh of the gods'. It is mined in the harsh quarries of the eastern desert, extracted from Nubia, extorted as tribute or retrieved as booty from foreign lands. Silver is much rarer and has been called the 'bones of the gods'. Most of it is imported from western Asia. Other precious materials, such as the blue stone lapis lazuli, come from as far away as Afghanistan and are obtained through trade.

Jewelry is universally popular and Egypt's many specialized craftsmen have mastered all aspects of its production. Beads and pendants of faïence (glazed ceramic) are produced in many hues and are quite affordable. On the luxury end of the scale are exquisite creations in gold and silver that can be embellished with beautiful stones such as carnelian and turquoise. Rings and beaded collars are quite fashionable, as are armlets, anklets and bracelets. Should you have the opportunity to watch some of the better Egyptian jewellers at work – perhaps even one of the pharaoh's own goldsmiths – you will witness a level of skill at work that will remain unsurpassed for thousands of years to come.

SANITATION

THE EGYPTIANS ARE AN exceptionally clean people. The average worker bathes at least once a day in the river or canal, or uses a jar of water as a sort of shower. Such cleanliness has its purpose. There are lots of flies and other disease-carrying nuisance insects that feed on garbage piles outside village homes, and fleas and lice are routine annoyances. Regular washing of body and clothes helps prevent disease, although parasitic worms and other nasty things are actually present in the Nile and other wash waters. Many Egyptians shave parts of their bodies for hygenic reasons and for some priests it serves as a purification ritual. Facial hair is unusual, although the pharaoh wears a false beard that serves as a symbol of kingship.

Take care while washing in the river or canal; parasites aren't the only creatures lurking unseen in the water. Crocodiles

THE LIFESPAN

The lifespan of the typical Egyptian worker is relatively short, between thirty and thirty-six years. Members of the upper classes, removed from the wear and tear of physical labour, can live decades longer. The present ruler, Ramesses II, for instance, has been on the throne for fifty-four years and is in his mid-seventies.

are common and occasionally enjoy the fortuitous treat of an inattentive bather.

MEDICAL EMERGENCIES

EVERY TRAVELLER HOPES TO AVOID disease and injury while on the road, or in this case, on the Nile. Realistically, though, there is always a risk of illness or accidental physical harm. But don't let this deter you: should you be so unlucky, help is available from Egyptian medical professionals.

The Egyptian physician is known as a *soonoo*. There's a hierarchy of these professionals, ranging from the local healers to those providing medical care for the pharaoh himself. Unless you're bringing in something new and exotic from the outside (which will be most unappreciated), Egyptian physicians will be aware of the symptoms of various common afflictions and injuries. With the empire's ongoing military adventures and big construction activities, they have centuries of experience in treating traumatic wounds. Dentists can be found here and there to take care of problems with your teeth and gums, and there are even specialist practitioners who address things such as gynaecological woes, snakebites and scorpion stings.

Should you need to visit a physician, don't be surprised if the doctor orders up an emetic to induce vomiting or some sort of enema concoction, or inserts a medicinal compound into one orifice or another to purge the body. The Egyptians believe that many illnesses are caused by the contaminating residues of internal bodily wastes. If you're suffering from one of the maladies common to many travellers, however, your body might already be purging itself on its own.

Egyptian medications are typically mixtures derived from a variety of plants, animals and minerals. Some include exotic ingredients such as mother's milk, urine from a virgin, excrement from flies, lizards, specific

---

RECIPE

Despite the fact that many Egyptians actually shave their heads, to serve the 'folically challenged', Egyptian physicians have developed the following recipe to cure baldness:

TO CAUSE HAIR TO GROW ON A BALD PERSON:

fat of lion, 1 [part];
fat of hippopotamus, 1 [part];
fat of crocodile, 1 [part];
fat of cat, 1 [part]; fat of snake, 1 [part];
fat of ibex, 1 [part];

make as one thing, smear (or anoint) the head of the bald person with it.

---

birds and crocodiles, blood from pigs and lizards, or perhaps a fried mouse. Many Egyptian practical remedies are also accompanied by magical incantations and spells, and in serious cases a priest might even be called in to invoke a deity associated with a particular affliction. Serket, for example, is a goddess who can be petitioned in the event of a scorpion sting. Her priests frequently serve as physicians and often prescribe a special Serket amulet for its curative powers.

THE COLOUR

The colour, substance and shape of various amulets usually have symbolic meanings. The metal gold, for example, can signify the concept of 'life' as nurtured by the sun; the red semi-precious stone carnelian represents the same concept as it is the colour of blood. If a natural material of the proper hue isn't available or is too expensive, a little ceramic glaze or paint in the appropriate colour will do the trick. Some amulets come in the shapes of certain animals, such as a lion or cobra, intended either to protect the wearer from the creature or to imbue him with desirable traits associated with the animal. One of the most powerful amulets of them all is the *udjat*, the protective 'Eye of Horus', which resembles the eye of a falcon and is worn by both the living and dead.

Speaking of protective amulets, you'll notice many Egyptians wearing them, even whole necklaces of them. Find yourself an amulet dealer and address your greatest fears. If you don't believe in their power, a wide selection of amulets will at least make for some attractive ethnic jewelry to show the folks back home.

THE RULES

UNDERSTANDING THE RULES OF behaviour in Egyptian culture will save you much grief and embarrassment. The Egyptians believe in a major cosmic concept that they call *maat*. *Maat*, which is often represented by a goddess with a feather on her head, is the abstract notion of truth and justice that is the ultimate goal of their stable society. The opposite of *maat* is chaos, something to be feared and utterly avoided. The pharaoh and priests make offerings to the gods in order to maintain their good will and beneficent assistance in sustaining cosmic *maat*, and individuals are expected to behave in a civil manner to promote *maat* in human society. At the most basic level, one should not murder, steal or cheat. Respect towards one's fellows, especially those of high rank, and respect of things sacred, including the ruler, are required. Your various inevitable minor mistakes in the way of social protocol will probably be ignored as something to be expected from an ignorant and uncouth outsider. However, as a foreigner you should try

The goddess Maat represents truth and cosmic order. The world is a better place when she is content.

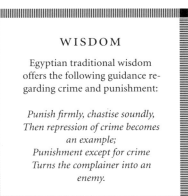

WISDOM

Egyptian traditional wisdom offers the following guidance regarding crime and punishment:

*Punish firmly, chastise soundly,
Then repression of crime becomes
an example;
Punishment except for crime
Turns the complainer into an
enemy.*

especially hard to conform to *maat*-like behaviour, as Egyptian ideology regards you as a symbol of chaos to be brought under control.

The Egyptians have courts staffed by officials who listen to various complaints and pass judgments. The cases heard range from property disputes to heinous criminal acts. Some crimes, such as minor theft, might be punished by a fine or a penalty of restitution, such as a repayment of the stolen goods at three times their value. On the other hand, one might be sentenced to a good old-fashioned beating with a whip or rod. One hundred lashes or strikes is not uncommon. For more serious crimes, one can be sent off to hard labour in the stone quarries or gold mines. Mutilations are occasionally prescribed, which can include cutting off the convicted criminal's nose or ears.

The very worst offenders, including those who plot against the king or desecrate sacred sites, might be awarded the

EXECUTION

Execution by burning is to be feared for reasons other than physical pain. The Egyptians believe that the body, even a dead one, houses manifestations of the soul. To reduce the body to nothing is to cause actual spiritual destruction; by being burned alive, one would essentially be obliterated to a state of nothingness.

[25]

death penalty by the pharaoh himself. The Egyptian style of execution is especially unpleasant and usually involves impalement or being burned alive.

Needless to say, as a foreigner, it's probably best not to stir up much controversy. Should you find yourself in serious legal trouble, banishment might be one of the more pleasant options for punishment; if this proves to be the case, accept the verdict with gratitude and proceed to the nearest border with all deliberate speed.

EGYPTIAN RELIGION

As you travel through Egypt, you'll quickly realize that religion permeates the entire culture. The Egyptians seem to have a spiritual relationship with nearly everything, including the divine king and the totality of nature as well as its individual parts. As a belief system, its complexity is staggering to the uninitiated. These are some of the basic characteristics of Egyptian religion and its practice, as graciously explained to the author by the high priest Khaemwaset, a leading scholar in the court of Ramesses II.

The Egyptians believe that there are divine forces at work everywhere and that different gods control nearly all aspects of their society. Each of these gods has specific characteristics and some are physically depicted in human form while others are shown as animals or animal–human hybrids. The foreigner might find the latter somewhat amusing (for example, the image of Thoth with his human body bearing the long-beaked head of an ibis bird, complete with a headdress, or the god Khepri, who has a scarab beetle for a head), but please don't laugh; most Egyptians take their religion seriously. The preponderance of deities is compounded by the melding of their characteristics into composite beings. The sun-god Ra, for example, is known as 'Ra-Khepri' in the morning, 'Ra-Harakhty' at noon, and 'Ra-Atum' in the evening. He is also worshipped as 'Amun-Ra', a composite deity combining the attributes of Ra with those of the god Amun.

The sun that shines bright and warm in the Egyptian sky plays a central role in the people's cosmological and religious beliefs. The Egyptians see the sun as a moving god who daily traverses a static sky, and descends into the west to the Netherworld beneath the earth to be reborn daily in the east, bringing warmth and light. There is a lingering fear that this process might stop – with catastrophic consequences – so solar worship and the proper personal and ritual behaviour of the pharaoh are considered essential. The movement of the sun is attributed to a giant pair of falcon wings, as embodied in the form of the sun-god known as Ra-Harakhty. The sun is sometimes also envisaged as a boat traversing the sky with a crew of gods, or as a searing golden ball being rolled across the heavens by a giant cosmic dung beetle.

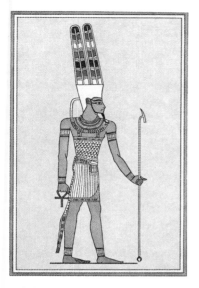

Behold! Amun-Ra, king of the gods.

ciated god by facilitating special burials for cats, falcons and even baboons.

Egyptian religion is practised on several different levels. At the lower tier, individuals might worship a particular god for its association with an occupation or for protection during a particular event such as childbirth. They might wear amulets representing the god or

Animal–god connections seem to be based on traits inherent in a particular creature. The goddesses Sekhmet and Paquet embody the fierce qualities of a lioness and the nocturnal desert habits of the jackal are expressed in the god Anubis who guards the cemeteries. You might find it surprising that the god Thoth is associated with both an ibis and a baboon. Remember, too, that some of the specific living animals that are venerated, such as the Apis bulls, are considered incarnations of a particular god which then inhabits another animal at the death of his current habitation. At some temples you might find people paying tribute to a specific animal-asso-

AMUN-RA

Amun-Ra is certainly the king of the gods during the time of Ramesses II. The following is an excerpt from a hymn in his honour:

Hail to thee, Amun-Ra,
Lord of the Thrones of the Two Lands,
Presiding over Karnak [the great
temple at Thebes],
Bull of His Mother, Presiding over His
Fields!
Far-reaching of stride, presiding over
Upper Egypt,
Lord of the Medjay and ruler of Punt
[southern foreign people and lands],
Eldest of heaven, first-born of earth,
Lord of what is, enduring in all things,
enduring in all things...

The gods fawn at his feet,
According as they recognize his majesty
as their lord,
The lord of fear, great of dread,
Rich in might, terrible of appearances,
Flourishing in offerings and making
provisions.
Jubilation to thee who made the gods,
Raised the heavens and laid down the
ground!

have a small shrine in the home. At the local level, each province has its own traditional patron god; some regions honour a triad of gods consisting of male and female consorts and an offspring. At Memphis, the triad consists of Ptah, Sekhmet and Nefertum; at Thebes, it's Amun and his spouse Mut along with their son, the moon-god Khonsu. On the national level there is the divine king, of course, and at present, a dominant king of the gods, Amun-Ra. (For a short descriptive list of some of the more prominent Egyptian gods, turn to the back of this book.)

GODS' MANSIONS AND GODS' SERVANTS

TEMPLES TO HONOUR AND SUSTAIN the gods are found scattered seemingly everywhere throughout Kemet, ranging in size from small shrines to gargantuan complexes covering many acres. These 'mansions of the gods' are sacred spaces that serve as theatres of ritual where offerings and other vital rites are conducted to nurture the benevolence of the divine. A content god is hopefully good to the people. Whatever its size, a temple will ultimately have some sort of shrine in its innermost chamber in which an image of a particular god is revered. One should keep in mind that it is not the cult statue itself that is being worshipped; the image only serves as an effective home for the god's spirits on earth.

The king is the supreme high priest, at

least theoretically, and is believed to be the divine intermediary between the people and the gods. Although the pharaoh occasionally does make a personal appearance in a temple to conduct the proper rituals, it's physically impossible for him actually to perform daily ceremonies in the numerous temples that theoretically require him. The temples, therefore, are staffed by a coterie of mostly full-time priests who perform these necessary duties on the pharaoh's behalf.

Being a priest is considered a prestigious if not lucrative job. There are several kinds, each with different roles and functions. Every temple has a chief priest, or 'god's servant', who alone is allowed to perform certain rituals pertaining to the cult statue and to visit it regularly. His job is particularly powerful: apart from controlling the sometimes substantial landholdings and other wealth of the temple, he is considered a prophet in the sense that he is allowed to interpret oracles and he sometimes speaks for the god in the first person.

The chief priest is assisted by *wab* ('clean' or 'pure') priests, whom you can recognize by their shaved heads and the braided sidelock otherwise typically worn by young boys. There are specialists, too, such as lector priests (*hery-hebet*), who read the rites during ceremonies, and *sem*-priests, who preside at funerals. The former have a reputation for being experts in magic and the latter are recognizable by a spotted leopard-skin draped across the shoulder.

[28]

Egyptian priests perform a variety of functions. A sem-*priest clad in a leopard skin, for example, presides at funeral services while a scroll-bearing lector priest reads the rites.*

There is also a whole category of *ka*-priests, who service the tombs of the deceased. Women are not a part of the priesthood per se, but some are employed in the prestigious roles of temple singers and musicians. Exceptionally, a woman – normally related to the royal family, sometimes by marriage – has the significant role of God's Wife of Amun, acting as the deity's consort in a ritual capacity.

From the little that is known to outsiders about the innermost activities of the temple, it seems that there are rituals that take place three times a day. In the morning, the chief priest unlocks the doors of the temple's shrine, and the god's image is cleaned and provided with fresh clothing. The god is then animated within the statue by conducting specific rites, and food and other offerings are presented for the god's sustenance and approval. The shrine is closed and sealed after the ritual, but approached twice more during the day. The offerings, of course, are not actually going to be consumed by an inanimate statue, so much of the high-quality food will be distributed among the priests – a substantial perk of the occupation.

As a foreigner, the extent to which you might visit any temple will be determined individually at each site. Some temple functionaries might ask you to go away while others might welcome you in an effort to show off the exterior beauty of the buildings or perhaps accept a 'donation' for a small peek inside. Even from the outside, though, these monuments to the gods are built to impress. Public access to most temples is usually confined to the outer courtyards, where you will be able to see common people bringing small stone tablets and other offerings, both beseeching and thanking the deity for answers to prayer.

AS WE PROGRESS...

YES, THERE IS MUCH TO LEARN in order to navigate the land of Egypt successfully and appreciate its culture, but we've barely started. Let's get on our way!

III · WELCOME TO EGYPT!

Two Lands and a River · Flora · Fauna
Communicating with the Locals: Language and Writing
Men-nefer (Memphis) Bound · Moving On…

IF YOU'VE SURVIVED THE TRIP TO Egypt and haven't been deported or imprisoned at entry, congratulations! The sites and culture of Kemet await, and the real adventure is just beginning. As you begin your journey up the Nile, some knowledge of Egypt's geography, flora and fauna, along with a few insights regarding communication, will help you appreciate the wonders you'll encounter on your journey.

TWO LANDS AND A RIVER

THE NILE RIVER IS AT THE CORE of Egypt's very existence. It delineates the country's borders and is responsible for the agricultural environment in which the people flourish. The Egyptians themselves call the river *itroo*, or simply, 'the river'.

The river originates in lands far to the south, and its two sources (the Blue Nile and the White Nile) eventually converge into a single stream in the land of Nubia. Flowing north, it passes through several turbulent rock stretches ('cataracts'), the most northerly serving as Egypt's southern border. From there the river travels through a broad valley, passing myriad villages and towns, along with important sites such as Waset (Thebes) and Abdju (Abydos). Not far from the

ancient capital of Men-nefer (Memphis), the river splits into several branches that feed a low expansive delta before emptying out into the Mediterranean Sea (which the Egyptians call *wadj-wer*, 'the great green'). From a poetic perspective, one might visualize the land of Egypt as resembling a beautiful lotus flower, with the long Nile Valley being its stem and the river's delta its bloom.

While having a major river pass through one's land by no means guarantees that a great civilization will arise, the natural cycle of the Nile certainly enhanced Egypt's capacity for food production, which allowed its civilization to develop and thrive. Every year, the river floods the lands along its banks, leaving deposits of nutrient-rich sediments. When the waters recede, the fields are wonderfully renewed.

COSMOLOGY

Egyptian cosmology holds that the earth is surrounded by waters above and below. With that world view, Egyptians believe that the Nile actually has its origins from these waters deep beneath the earth.

NILE FLOODS

Although Egypt's reputation as a 'breadbasket' is well known and refugees from neighbouring regions often come to Egypt seeking relief from drought, the Egyptians have not always been protected from such catastrophes. The Nile can flood too much and cause extensive damage, or worse, not rise sufficiently. Measuring devices (which the Greeks will call 'Nilometers') can be found here and there on the Nile to track the river's levels.

The Nile river provides a marvellous natural highway, its waters plied by an immense number of boats of all kinds.

observed at work on the river, from small fishing skiffs made from bundles of papyrus to large wooden barges capable of transporting immense blocks of

HAPI

The Egyptians worship a god of the Nile inundation called Hapi. Hapi is typically depicted as a man with a fat belly and pendulous breasts, blue skin and aquatic plants sprouting from the top of his head. Given the importance of a healthy yet restrained annual flooding of the river, one can see why the Egyptians believe in such a god and plead for his goodwill in the form of a perfectly balanced inundation. Hapi is said to lurk in a cave somewhere near the first cataract at Egypt's southern border.

The river also very importantly serves as a highway – and an especially good one at that. Its natural flowing course allows watercraft to travel easily with the current from south to north. Fortuitously, the prevailing winds of Egypt blow from the opposite direction, the north, allowing boats to raise their sails and make their way upstream. Watercraft of all sizes and function can be

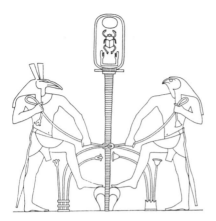

stone. In between are a variety of vessels, including domestic ferries, naval ships and commercial boats sailing off on missions with trading partners in the eastern Mediterranean.

Egypt is divided into two main regions based on the flow of the river. The Nile Valley is referred to as Upper Egypt (upstream) and the Delta as Lower Egypt (downstream). Given that the Nile Valley stretches for hundreds of miles, it's sometimes useful for the traveller to subdivide Upper Egypt with the artificial designation of 'Middle Egypt' extending south from Memphis to around Thebes. (See Chapter VII.)

The Egyptians are acutely aware of the Upper Egypt–Lower Egypt geographical distinction, and it has vitally shaped their history. Long ago, the two regions were separate political entities and periodically warred with each other. Around 2,000 years before Ramesses' reign, conflict between the two sides came to an end with the victory of a ruler of Upper

Egypt whom the Egyptians remember as 'Menes'. Menes is credited with the unification of the two regions and the establishment of the original Egyptian state from which the present civilization arose and developed. Even now, the importance of the unified land is continually emphasized at the royal level. The ruler of Egypt bears the titles of King of Upper and Lower Egypt and Lord of the Two Lands. In Egyptian art, and on ceremonial occasions, the pharaoh wears a red crown representing Lower Egypt, a white crown representing Upper Egypt or, perhaps more frequently, a combined double crown expressing his sovereignty over both regions. He might also sport a headdress held in place by a diadem bearing a likeness of Wadjet, the Lower Egyptian cobra goddess, or Nekhbet, the Upper Egyptian vulture goddess, or both of them. The two lands are separated into forty-two provinces: twenty-two in Upper Egypt and twenty in Lower Egypt. These provinces have played various roles in Egyptian history, some serving as power centres or having special relationships between each other as allies or enemies. Each has a chief town or city and a patron god or gods.

Leaving the Nile region and venturing off to the west and east, one will find vast deserts whose arid expanses serve as natural barriers. However, these desolate territories are not necessarily without value. To the east there are a number of stone quarries, gold mines and other mineral resources that provide the rulers of Egypt with wealth and building mate-

KEEPING HAPI HAPPY

The Egyptians have every reason to keep Hapi happy and the following ingratiating hymn to the Nile god clearly expresses their appreciation:

Praise to you, O Nile, that issues from the earth, and comes to nourish Egypt…
That waters the fields that Ra has created to nourish all cattle,
That gives drink to the desert places which are from water,
That makes barley and creates wheat, so that he may cause the temples to keep festivals…
When he rises, the land is in exultation and everybody is in joy…
He that brings victuals and is rich in food, that creates all that is good.

rials. A few cross-country routes traverse this eastern desert from the Nile Valley to the Red Sea, where expeditions to exotic lands are launched and return.

In the west, there are several oases requiring a number of days of desert travel to reach them. Although not rich in minerals or stone, these sparsely populated oases produce tasty dates and olives and some of the better wines in Egypt. In the western deserts one can also find some arduous caravan routes

venturing north to south allowing one to bypass the Nile Valley if so desired.

The fertile region ('the Fayyum') is found just south-west of Memphis bordering the western desert. The area features a large lake whose waters and marshy surroundings are popular for hunting and fishing. A favourite deity of the region, the crocodile god Sobek, reminds the local inhabitants that not all of the wildlife in the lake is easily hunted – some of it actually does the hunting.

OPPOSITE: *The nasty god Seth and his heroic nephew Horus are reconciled in this symbolic depiction of the united Upper and Lower Egypt. At the top of the pillar is the hieroglyphic name of a ruler of the Two Lands.*

RIGHT: *The shores of the Nile teem with plant and animal life.*

Some of the lovely water plants found along the Nile's banks include papyrus and lotus.

FLORA

A S YOU SOJOURN ALONG THE Nile, you'll notice that the banks and shallow waters are crowded with greenery: reeds, rushes, sedges and the all-important papyrus for which Egypt is famous. This versatile plant grows up to 16 feet in height and is crowned by a decorative spray of fine green filaments. Apart from being a source-material for the production of paper, this fibrous plant can be manipulated into ropes, baskets and even sandals. Its roots are said to be edible but are not a popular food choice unless one is desperately hungry. Floating here and there in the water you will no doubt notice the lotus, with their flat green leaves and beautiful flowers in both blue and white varieties.

On both sides of the river, much of the plant-life that dominates the countryside is, of course, emmer wheat, barley and flax, which are the mainstays of Egyptian agriculture, along with various vegetable crops. Although you'll find little in Egypt that resembles a 'forest', there are clumps, groves and individual trees of several species dotting the landscape. The sycamore fig, for example, spreads its leafy branches to provide welcome shade and tasty fruit. There are also plenty of thorny-branched acacia trees with leaves and seeds that are munched by cattle. Its wood is commonly converted into planks for use in furniture, boats and coffins. The acacia also produces a resinous gum that can be used as a binding agent. Other common trees are tamarisks, willows, olives and the thorn bush, which is an indigenous hardwood. Out in the desert fringes grows the moringa tree, highly valued for its natural oils.

The majestic, striking palms are among the most useful and versatile trees that grow in Egypt. The trunks can be used for roofing and other building functions and the stems and leaves of the fronds have seemingly endless uses in making baskets, mats and crates, among other things. The date palm, of course, is valued for its delicious fruit, which you should definitely sample. Another palm, the dom, is distinctive in that its trunk forks into branches and it produces a large, hard nut.

Despite all of its greenery, Egypt really doesn't have the quantity of wood that it needs, and a great deal of timber is imported from other lands. High-quality wood that is capable of producing wide planks has long been brought in from regions to the east, especially Phoenicia with its huge cedar trees that grow on inland slopes. Yew, juniper, fir and cypress are also valuable foreign woods. If you're travelling up the Nile by wooden boat, and you probably are, take a look at how these vessels are put together. Many seem to be composed of odd pieces of wood, shaped to fit, tied together with rope and then caulked. Don't be alarmed – this method of construction is a skilled Egyptian art, and it's perfectly watertight. Some furniture, too, is made from whatever wood scraps are available and then expertly assembled with mortise-and-tenon techniques.

The Egyptians appreciate natural beauty wherever it is found and especially love flowers, which are often woven into collars or combined into bouquets for celebrations. The lotus, in particular, is valued not only for its beauty and aroma, but also for its alleged narcotic qualities, which are said to spice up a party, especially when mixed with alcohol.

FAUNA

THE EGYPTIANS SHARE THEIR world with an abundant and diverse collection of animal life, some of which are useful and cherished and others dreaded and feared. At the smaller end of the scale are insects, including the honeybee (the symbol of Lower Egypt), the annoying fly (which you'll get to know quite well during your visit), and the dung- or scarab beetle. The dangerous scorpion, whose sting can cause severe illness or death, hides under rocks or in other dark places during the day: another reason to avoid walking barefoot through the desert. Their swiftness and power so impressed the early Egyptians that at least one of the earliest kings was named 'Scorpion'. To avoid meeting the legendary king's namesake, it's a good idea to shake out your clothes or empty beer jugs before you use either.

Frogs are abundant in Egypt and are a symbol of fertility as they produce offspring in huge quantities, so much so that in the Egyptian writing system a tadpole represents the numeral 100,000. Similarly, the Egyptian word for 'many' is written with a hieroglyph depicting a lizard: the Egyptians don't particularly like lizards but there are plenty of them in the country.

There are over thirty kinds of snakes in Egypt, some of which are harmless and others that are deadly poisonous. Egyptian physicians are aware of the toxicity of each species and have ways of treating bites that they consider survivable. There is a snake god, Apophis, who is considered the enemy of order and stability and therefore must be neutralized. On the other hand, Wadjet, the protective cobra goddess of Lower Egypt, is represented by the *uraeus* symbol, often

The lowly scarab beetle serves as a powerful symbol
of regeneration, as expressed in these popular amulets – which make great souvenirs.

THE SCARAB

Strange as it may seem to revere an animal that flourishes in excrement, the scarab or dung beetle has a special place in Egyptian mythology. The beetles feed on manure and lay their eggs in dung that they roll in front of them, producing a roundish ball, which is then deposited in an underground den. The developing beetles eventually eat their way out of the balls, creating the illusion that they have been spontaneously generated. The scarab, with its round moving dung ball, has therefore come to represent regeneration, especially in association with the rising orb of the sun represented by the god Khepri. Small stone or faïence amulets in the shape of scarabs with flat bases are popular among the Egyptians. Some bear good-luck mottos or are inscribed with the names and titles of officials for use as a seal. Large inscribed scarabs have been produced by some pharaohs to commemorate special events.

found on royal diadems and head-dresses. For the traveller, it's best to assume that all snakes in Egypt are poisonous and keep your distance.

Big cats such as lions survive here and there in the wilderness fringes. Your chances of seeing these over-hunted and therefore increasingly rare animals are remote; but out in the desert you're quite likely to encounter antelope, ibex and gazelles, which are pursued for sport and admired for their rugged grace. Nocturnal jackals and red foxes roam the arid hills and hyenas are hunted in the edges of the desert. The *ichneumon*, or mongoose, can be seen scurrying through the countryside hunting mice and snakes, earning the gratitude of the human population.

There are, of course, the domesticated creatures, including cattle, sheep and goats, pigs, donkeys and horses, that serve the needs of humans. A few varieties of geese and ducks are widely domesticated and quail and migratory game birds are frequently captured. In terms of pets, the Egyptians are rather fond of dogs and have developed several breeds. Dogs are often appreciated for

Beware! Wild and often dangerous animals lurk in the desert and other fringe wilderness areas.

their hunting skills and are cherished companions; unlike most animals in Egypt, they are sometimes given personal names. Cats, too, are very well liked. A prince of Amenhotep III is said to have buried his beloved female cat in an appropriately-sized inscribed stone sarcophagus that would have done a noble lady proud. Some members of the elite also keep imported monkeys as pets, apparently finding these creatures' unpredictable antics amusing. You might be tempted to pet these little furry fellows or even buy one in a market, but be warned that the novelty wears off quickly: monkeys can be very obnoxious and they do bite.

A large number of birds can be found along Egypt's marshes and fields. Particularly eye-catching are the long-beaked ibis, visiting lapwings and the hoopoe with its feather-crested head. Common raptors include hawks, owls and vultures.

ANIMAL SOUNDS

Egyptian language possesses a number of sounds and words that are imitative of animals. The word for 'cat' is *mioo*, 'pig' is *reree* and 'donkey' is *a-aa*. The hieroglyph that represents the sound 'f' is symbolized by the horned viper. This deadly snake makes a rustling noise that sounds like *ffffffff* as it prepares to fling itself at its victim.

Two of the most dangerous creatures to be found in Egypt lurk in the river and swamps: the hippopotamus and the crocodile. Hippos and crocodiles have few natural enemies – other than each other – and either is capable of winning a stand-off. Hippos are highly feared by the Egyptians, who recognize their phys-

Don't be fooled by the comical appearance of the hippopotamus. It is one of the most dangerous and aggressive creatures found in Egypt.

WEBAONER

There's an old Egyptian story about a priest named Webaoner whose wife was having an illicit affair with a man from town. A servant reported this activity and Webaoner engaged in a little Egyptian magic by fashioning a small crocodile made of wax that the servant could place in the water when his wife's boyfriend went to bathe. When the time came, the wax crocodile turned into the real thing and a large one at that. The crocodile grabbed the man and held him underwater for seven days. Webaoner took the pharaoh to see the results of this impressive bit of sorcery and the crocodile reverted once again to its wax form before being released into the Nile. The unfaithful wife was burned and her body thrown into the river.

local habitats of these creatures while visiting areas near water. In general, do avoid falling into the Nile, especially near shore.

Hippos are occasionally hunted by the divinely robust pharaoh and the ivory from their teeth is also highly valued. Other, more exotic animals – including monkeys, baboons, leopards, cheetahs, giraffes and even rhinoceros – are sometimes imported from Nubia or more distant lands for their by-products or novelty value. Even live bears have been brought in from lands east. Some of Egypt's rulers, especially Hatshepsut, Thutmose III and the present Ramesses, have been particularly fond of collecting foreign animals and have set up small zoos, often planted with exotic imported trees.

COMMUNICATING WITH THE LOCALS: LANGUAGE AND WRITING

AS A VISITOR TO EGYPT, IT'S unlikely that you will understand much of the language. If you travelled by way of Canaan, there's a good chance that you heard it spoken by some of the soldiers, tribute collectors or other Egyptian citizens living there; if you came by ship from the eastern Mediterranean ports, you may have heard some of it spoken by sailors and merchants. For most foreign visitors, Egyptian is so different from their own languages that it is essentially unintelligible.

Don't panic. Because of Egypt's interest in international trade and empire

ical power and aggressiveness. Don't be fooled by their awkward girth or by the cuteness of the young ones; hippos are capable of overturning small boats and inflicting mortal wounds with their large tusks and crushing bite. Crocodiles require little explanation. They can quietly hide in waiting only to leap out and grab an unsuspecting bather, laundress, or foreign visitors – they don't discriminate. The victim is typically pulled underwater and drowned prior to being devoured. Make enquiries about the

It takes years of training to master the Egyptian hieroglyphic and cursive scripts – just ask this happy scribe!

building, there are a good number of translators and scribes in the land. You will no doubt meet some of them when you are questioned as you enter the country. You will also probably find some bilingual foreigners living in Egypt, in merchant colonies, as diplomats, or as prisoners of war. Although the language might at first seem intimidating, simply recognize it for what it is: just another of the many languages you don't know.

One aspect of language and culture that can be very baffling to visitors is the Egyptian writing system. At first appearance, it seems to be a random assortment of hundreds of pictures representing an enormous range of subjects: animals, people, household goods, boats and plants, along with many symbols that are utterly unidentifiable at first glance. One's first assumption might be that all these signs are actually a form of picture-writing in which a story can be read by interpreting the individual figures as images in a message. A couple of birds followed by a man with a stick, you might surmise, is some sort of hunting story. If you have heard rumours about the Egyptians and all their esoteric beliefs, you might conjecture that these 'hieroglyphs' are some sort of mystical rambling. Neither of these assumptions is true. Most of the Egyptian writing system, as in other languages, simply represents the sounds of their speech in visible form, albeit a very complicated one. Yes, it actually is a script that can be read, written and understood by someone who has been properly trained.

The simplest of all writing systems would involve a script in which one symbol represents one sound in the language (an 'alphabet'). In the time of Ramesses II, however, there are very few languages written this way, and the Egyptian system is much more complicated. Although it does include alphabetic characters, which one might think would suffice, there are also symbols that stand for combinations of two or three consonants and numerous others that have no sound value whatsoever. These latter symbols, however, are especially useful in helping one determine the meaning of the word in this script, as the vowel sounds are generally not indicated.

During your visit, you'll see the Egyptian script in its most glorious form on mighty statues to Ramesses and his predecessors and on the towering walls of temples to the gods. Carved in stone,

HIEROGLYPHIC SCRIPT

While one may be dismayed by the cumbersome nature of the Egyptian hieroglyphic script, one need not look outside the general region to find writing systems of at least equal complexity. In Mesopotamia, the Sumerians, Akkadians and Babylonians developed a script consisting of hundreds of groupings of wedged-shaped ('cuneiform') symbols that represent combinations of consonants and vowels. To the untrained eye, these symbols can truly appear nearly identical, if not outright confusing. Documents in the cuneiform script are typically written on clay tablets on which the symbols are impressed with a reed stylus.

these inscriptions will likely survive for thousands of years to confuse and enlighten future generations. Should you manage to have some of these royal monumental texts translated for you, expect shameless propaganda: the enhancement of the pharaoh's reputation tends to be the norm. On at least six temples in Egypt and Nubia, for example, the great martial feats of Ramesses II in a battle with the Hittites at Kadesh in Syria are proclaimed both visually and in text:

The stand which his majesty made while he was camping on the north-west of Kadesh. He charged into the midst of the foe belonging to the vanquished chief of Kheta (Hittites), while he was alone by himself, and no

If you believe the propaganda, Ramesses II is an army unto himself.

other with him. *He found surrounding him 2,500 horses in four bodies on his every side. He slaughtered them, making them heaps underneath his horses. He slew all the chiefs of all the countries, the allies of the vanquished chiefs of Kheta, together with his own great chiefs, his infantry and his chariotry. He overthrew them prostrate upon their faces, and hurled them down, one upon another into the waters of the Orontes [a river in Syria]. His majesty was behind them like a fierce-eyed lion…*

Now either Ramesses is indeed some sort of mighty superhero, or there's something not quite accurate here. (In reality the great battle resulted in a draw.) While in Egypt, it's probably best

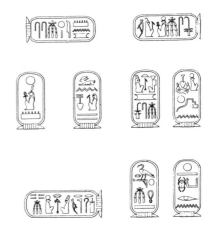

The names of Egyptian rulers are written with hieroglyphs in elongated circles. It's a good way to tell who built what – or usurped it.

PAPER

The manufacture of paper from the papyrus plant is truly a great invention. Unlike the clunky clay tablets, pottery scraps and discarded flakes of stone used in other parts of the ancient world, paper is light, durable and easily rolled into scrolls of any desired length. Stripping away the green outer skin of a papyrus stalk reveals a whitish, pithy interior that can be cut into thin strips and laid out in an overlapping pattern. Under prolonged compression, natural adhesives produce a bonding effect resulting in a sheet of paper of great versatility.

to be diplomatic and at least pretend that their official version is true. Practise looking suitably impressed.

By the way, it's relatively easy to identify for whom a monument has been built. Look among the hieroglyphs for oval-shaped symbols that enclose script. These ovals ('cartouches' in much later parlance) represent a symbol for eternity. Royal names are typically found in pairs, representing the ruler's two primary names.

Apart from carefully carved texts on formal monuments, the Egyptians produce a paper from the papyrus plant that is ideally suited for the writing of everyday documents. The paper is light, durable and easily rolled into scrolls of any desired length. A cursive derivative of the formal hieroglyphic script is used to write on this paper with pens produced from reeds and a palette of black and red ink. Very few people in Egypt can read and write, other than educated members of the upper echelons of society and rigorously trained scribes. The job of a scribe is therefore very prestigious.

MEN-NEFER (MEMPHIS) BOUND

LET'S DO SOME TRAVELLING! There are several choices of itineraries, but the routes all follow the Nile upstream. Even if you're sufficiently unsettled at the border to want to turn and run, at least venture to the ancient city of Men-nefer (Memphis) with its cosmopolitan atmosphere and nearby pyramids. Those who really wish to experience the greatness of Egypt should definitely carry on to Waset (Thebes). There are many wonderful things to see along the way and the magnificence of the Theban monuments is unparalleled. Those with greater ambition might choose to continue to Egypt's southern border, where an excursion into Nubia awaits the very bold adventurer.

If you've arrived in Egypt via the Ways of Horus, you'll be greeted by a dazzling example of Egypt's might and wealth soon after you leave the intimidating fortress of Tjaru. Not far away is the magnificent new city of Pi-Ramesses, the present pharaoh's royal residence. To get there, you'll need to cross the branch of the Nile called 'The Waters of Ra', named for the Egyptian sun-god. If you're coming by sea, it's likely that you'll be making your arrival at the busy inland river port, where you, your shipmates and accompanying cargo will be assessed. Pi-Ramesses is a must-see stop and a great spot for you to rest after your long journey. Find a place to stay and visit for a few days as you get a first up-close glimpse of the land's grandeur.

Pi-Ramesses, more formally, Pi-Ramesses, Aa-Nakhtu (House of Ramesses, Great of Victories) is situated in the vicinity of the old Hyksos capital of Avaris. Ramesses II's father, Seti, built a lovely summer palace here, which his son has expanded into a magnificent, important and thriving city, pleasantly situated between the desert frontier and the lush agricultural fields with the Nile at their edge. The city is also strategically located to serve as a departure point for military expeditions to parts east and as a reception area and storage depot for foreign wealth through commerce, tribute or booty. The surrounding waters of the Nile provide defence and security.

Pi-Ramesses is indeed a lovely place, as a scribe named Pibesa has described it:

It is a fair spot, there is not the like of it; resembling Thebes, it was Ra who found it himself. The Residence [city of the king] is agreeable to live in, its fields are full of all good things;...abundance of food is in it every day; one rejoices to dwell within it, no wish is left by it to be spoken.

Ramesses II has greatly expanded his father's palace, adorning it with luxurious interiors featuring coloured glazed tiles. Don't count on seeing much of it unless you're a supremely important individual or employed within 'The Residence'. As an ordinary visitor, however, you'll still be impressed by the exterior of the palace and the city's other attractions, such as its temples. Many of the city's inhabitants are bureaucrats and others who support the government's various functions. Their roles and titles are numerous and they and the royal household are supported by a huge number of domestic servants and workers of all sorts employed to keep the administration functioning and the privileged comfortable.

The royal city is an animated place. If you walk through its streets during morning hours, you will see a crosssection of Egyptian society going about its business: impeccably-dressed officials in starched white tunics and skirts making their way to their offices, temple-bound priests recognizable by their shiny bald heads, household servants scurrying about to fulfil the needs of their well-off bosses and nearly naked slaves tediously labouring at menial tasks. Farmers on the city's outskirts work their fields and vendors sit on the dusty streets selling produce and wares exhibited in woven baskets and clay pots.

Make sure you visit the busy port. This city is a centre for the importation of much of the fruits of Egypt's empire and your senses will be stimulated as exotic goods from the east and elsewhere are unloaded and distributed from welltravelled ships.

BUILDING MATERIALS

The Nile Delta contains few rock outcroppings suitable for quarrying, so most of the high-quality stone found in the temples, palaces and other monuments in that region is imported from sources that are sometimes hundreds of miles away. The downstream currents of the Nile make possible the movement of stone-laden barges. Ramesses II himself is said to have selected some of the stone used for statues in his royal city. Other building materials are obtained by stripping away the sites of earlier towns or monuments (the Hyksos capital of Avaris, for example). Given this practice, it's unlikely that much will be left of Pi-Ramesses centuries from now.

There are several splendid temples to be seen in Pi-Ramesses, some equipped with multiple pairs of stone obelisks and columned halls and dedicated to popular gods such as Amun and Ptah. You might be allowed in the outermost courtyard of these temples, if you show proper respect, but access to the gates, courts and chambers beyond becomes progressively more exclusive, even among the priestly hierarchy.

Look for the spectacular 'jubilee halls' of the pharaoh among the royal and religious structures. Periodically the long-lived Ramesses performs an ancient ceremony to renew and celebrate his kingship. It's known as the *sed*-festival and it involves a series of highly symbolic rites that proclaim the pharaoh's legitimacy as Lord of the Two Lands while demonstrating his physical prowess and fitness to rule. As you roam about the temples and other monuments, you'll notice many dozens of statues of Ramesses II, finely rendered in stone, typically larger than life, with a few being utterly colossal. Get used to them – they will become a very common sight as you continue your journey through Egypt.

While you might be enamoured of the city's beauty, vigour and regal splendour, you may also sense sinister military undertones in its atmosphere. Hundreds of sturdy horses, chariots and their drivers reside here and garrisons of soldiers await their battle orders. You might notice the acrid smell of iron furnaces with which skilled smiths manufacture weapons. Other equipment specialists, too, are hard at work supplying the troops that will leave and return by the same route you will: via the nearby Ways of Horus or by ship from the city's great port.

MOVING ON...

Pᴵ-ʀᴀᴍᴇssᴇs ɪs ɪɴᴅᴇᴇᴅ ᴀ dramatic introduction to Egypt but eventually you'll want to leave its many charms and move on south. It shouldn't be too difficult to find a local ferry or commercial boat departing from the city's river port and travelling down the Waters of Ra in the direction of Memphis. Depending on the wind, the journey will probably take only five days to a week. Along the way your ship might stop here and there, perhaps

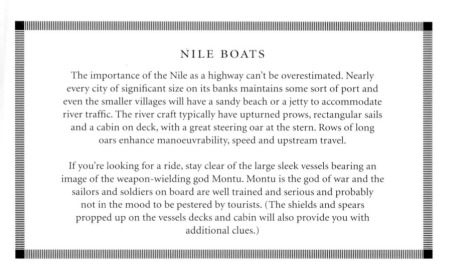

NILE BOATS

The importance of the Nile as a highway can't be overestimated. Nearly every city of significant size on its banks maintains some sort of port and even the smaller villages will have a sandy beach or a jetty to accommodate river traffic. The river craft typically have upturned prows, rectangular sails and a cabin on deck, with a great steering oar at the stern. Rows of long oars enhance manoeuvrability, speed and upstream travel.

If you're looking for a ride, stay clear of the large sleek vessels bearing an image of the weapon-wielding god Montu. Montu is the god of war and the sailors and soldiers on board are well trained and serious and probably not in the mood to be pestered by tourists. (The shields and spears propped up on the vessels decks and cabin will also provide you with additional clues.)

doing a bit of trading, taking on and letting off passengers, or even anchoring or coming to shore every evening. Don't worry about the time; it took you long enough to get this far and a reasonable tour through Egypt will require at least several weeks. Relax and enjoy the beautiful green fields, the bucolic scenes of the local people at work and the waterfowl along the river's banks as you steadily sail upstream beneath Egypt's shining sun.

Proceeding south, a couple of interesting places can be found along the way. The city of Per-Bastet (Bubastis) is a cult centre for the worship of the protective cat-goddess Bastet. If you happen to be passing by when the very popular Bastet festival is in full session, you might want to stop for a visit. The festival is known for its joyous atmosphere with lots of music, drinking and dancing, as the Greek historian Herodotus will later report:

When the people are on their way to Bubastis they go by river…a great number in every boat. Some of the women make a noise with rattles, others play flutes all the way, while the rest of the women, and the men, sing and clap their hands…whenever they come near any other town, they bring their boat near the bank; then some of the women…shout mockery of the women of the town; others dance, and others stand up and expose their persons. This they do whenever

DEITIES

According to Egyptian mythology there were four pairs of deities before the world was created. There are several different versions of the creation story, but in one particularly prominent account, the god Atum emerged from a mound of slime and proceeded to generate other vital gods and cosmic entities. Atum first created Shu (air) and his consort Tefnut (moisture). Then came Geb (earth) and Nut (sky). The rest of the universe was made from these four components. Geb and Nut produced two pairs of male and female divine offspring: Osiris and Isis, along with Seth and Nephthys.

Following the creation, the divine extended family began to squabble, with a feud between Seth and Osiris, the murder and mutilation of Osiris by Seth, and the revitalization of Osiris as king of the Netherworld of the deceased. Horus, the son of Osiris, and Isis successfully took revenge against Seth and today the Egyptians believe that Horus is incarnated within the living ruler of Egypt (although it's doubtful that you'll ever see Ramesses flitting through the sky with a genuine falcon head). As far as the origins of people are concerned, a favourite belief is that the talented ram-headed god Khnum fashions individuals and their spirits on a potter's wheel. There are several million people in Egypt, so he must be busy.

they come beside any riverside town. But when they reached Bubastis, they make a festival with great sacrifices, and more wine is drunk at this feast than in the whole year beside. Men and women (but not children) are wont to assemble there to the number of 700,000, as the people of the place say.

Further down the river you will find Nay-Ta-Hut (Yehudiya), which was once a city of the despised Hyksos but is now a thriving reoccupied town.

CITY OF THE SUN

A**PPROXIMATELY FOUR DAYS' SAIL** south from Pi-Ramesses, you can take a canal from the river to visit what is certainly one of the largest cities in all of Egypt: Iunu (Heliopolis). Iunu is arguably the original spiritual capital of Egypt and is a major ancient centre of solar worship, astronomy and several interesting cults. Herodotus will later report that 'the people of Heliopolis are said to be the most learned of the Egyptians'. There you will find a temple to Ra in his manifestation as the god of the sun, 'Ra-Harakhty', rising prominently on the horizon. From the canal, you can pick out the temple in the city-scape by locating its several pairs of obelisks, mighty stone pillars reaching into the sky, their gilded summit pyramidions gleaming. The obelisks have been donated by past royal luminaries, including the pharaohs Senusert I and Thutmose III, and they give the city its Egyptian name, Iunu, which means 'pillar'.

Obelisks are dramatic symbols of a solar cult as well as masterpieces of Egyptian stone-cutting.

OBELISKS

Obelisks are tapered rectangular pillars whose tops terminate in the form of a pyramid (called a pyramidion). Related to the cult of the sun, these stone monuments can be as much as 90 feet tall and are typically adorned with dedicatory hieroglyphic inscriptions. Carving, transporting and erecting a large obelisk is a major engineering feat. What would have been the largest obelisk of them all, at about 130 feet tall, can be seen still in a granite quarry at Sunu (Aswan) near Egypt's southern border, where it cracked in place before it could be removed.

The Iunu shrine dedicated to Atum is especially noteworthy as it is purported to be located on the very site where the Egyptian creator god emerged from a primeval hill of slime and proceeded to create the other gods, who brought the world into being. Located on a bit of high ground, its open courtyard houses the *benben*-stone: a short, squat gold-tipped obelisk that marks the spot of the creation and captures the rays of the sun. You will find cult centres in the city for the worship of sacred trees and a bull-god, Mer-wer, who is associated with the sun. In the latter case, the god is represented by a single black, virile, living bull who is pampered in life and buried with great ceremony in death and then replaced by another living black bull incarnating Mer-wer. There are other religious festivals from time to time that you might find intriguing, including several that celebrate various phases of the lunar month.

If your foreign eyes find Iunu grand and mysterious, if not a little on the bizarre side, brace yourself – there's more, a whole lot more, ahead.

OTHER INTERESTING SITES

Should you find yourself entering Egypt from the north-western branches of the Nile, you'll miss the spectacular cities of Pi-Ramesses and Iunu. No need to be dismayed: there are other interesting sites to see in this region as you make your way south towards Memphis. The city of Per-Wadjet (Buto) was an early capital of Lower Egypt and features a temple to the cobra goddess Wadjet. Be wary: her local popularity might be due to the ubiquity of cobras in the area.

Another city, Sa-u (Sais) is a major cult centre for the worship of the aggressive warrior-goddess Neith – who, curiously enough, is also the patroness of hunting and weaving – and is certainly worthy of a visit.

PRECEDING PAGES:
I Although he is getting on in years, hundreds of colossal statues proclaim the youthful strength and vitality of Ramesses II.
II Nile boats come in all sizes. The river currents aid northerly travel and hoisting a sail will ease the journey south. A little paddling helps.

THIS PAGE:
III In Egypt, cattle represent wealth. Private, royal and religious estates all own large numbers of them. Here an overseer counts his master's wealth.

OPPOSITE:
IV Egyptians know how to throw a party and talented musicians are often part of the festivities. If you're lucky, someone might give you a lotus flower to sniff.
V Bread, along with beer, is an Egyptian staple. Having a little model of bread-makers in one's tomb ensures an ample supply until the end of time.

FOLLOWING PAGES:
VI *What do Egyptians expect in the afterlife? Much of the same that they experienced in life, but without the pain. In this scene from a nobleman's tomb, the deceased barely breaks a sweat as he ploughs a field while his wife, wearing an expensive linen dress, sows seeds.*

VII Those under the far-reaching authority of Egypt are expected to show homage to the ruler, including these emissaries from Nubia bearing tribute.

IV · CAPITAL ATTRACTIONS

Welcome to Memphis • Pharaoh Almighty
Ramesses the Great Himself • All the King's Men
The Military • The Memphis Experience

WELCOME TO MEMPHIS

WHATEVER YOUR AMBITIONS IN exploring Egypt, a visit to Memphis, or in Egyptian parlance, Inbuhedj, is essential. There you will find the city that is at Kemet's core, a cosmopolitan cultural hub with thick historical roots that remains at least the sentimental capital of the land. It's situated about 20 miles south of Iunu (Heliopolis) and, depending on the winds, perhaps less than a day's sail upstream. Inbuhedj means 'white walls' and refers to the gleaming façade of the ancient capital's royal palace. The city also goes by the name Men-nefer meaning 'enduring in beauty', an appellation borrowed from the nearby pyramid of Pepi I. The city really has endured: it dates back to the first king of Egypt, Menes, and the establishment of the unified Egyptian state around 2,000 years ago. As the Two Lands' first capital, its strategic location was essential to its success, situated as it is just south of where the Nile splits into branches that feed the Delta, and accessible to desert caravan routes. Memphis is also the city of the god Ptah, a patron deity of craftsmen whom some credit with the creation of the world.

One might argue that the political, religious and cultural dominance of this sprawling city has been eclipsed over the

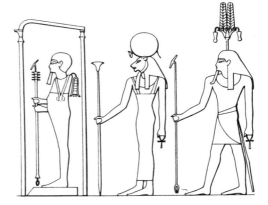

The triad of gods favoured in Memphis consists of Ptah with his tight blue cap, his fierce lioness wife Sekhmet, and their dapper son Nefertum, who is the god of perfume.

[57]

last few centuries by Waset (Thebes) to the south, and over the last few decades by the new capital of Pi-Ramesses to the north-east. Not necessarily so. Memphis continues to hold its own and still remains one of Egypt's most important cities. The city's major port serves as a central distribution centre for much of Egypt. In its vicinity you will find visiting merchants and colonies of foreigners providing goods and services to this dynamic land. Walk among the markets and wharfs and you'll hear many exotic languages as ships load and unload their cargo under the watchful eyes of Egyptian assessors. You might be surprised to find some of these outsiders freely worshipping Asiatic deities such as Baal and Astarte, which are tolerated, if not respected and occasionally even revered by some of the Egyptians, although Ptah, with his tight blue cap and tightly grasped sceptre, remains unmistakably dominant here.

Apart from the markets and ports, the sites of Memphis, like so many other interesting places in Egypt, are mostly of the royal and religious variety. The white-walled palace and its accompanying staff are still quite active, awaiting the return of Ramesses as he occasionally travels about the land. Don't expect to see anything more than its exterior, but you'll still marvel at what can be done architecturally with mud bricks, stone and wood.

A POEM

The emotional attraction of Memphis for Egyptians is expressed in this poem by a young student longing to return home.

Oh, I'm bound downstream on the Memphis ferry,
like a runaway, snapping all ties,
With my bundle of old clothes over my shoulder.

I'm going down there where the living is,
going down there to that big city,
And I'll tell Ptah (Lord who loves justice):
'Give me a girl tonight!'…

…And the quiet joy of tomorrow,
dawn whitening over her loveliness:
O, Memphis, my city, beauty forever! –
You are a bowl of love's own berries,
Dish set for Ptah your god,
god of the handsome face.

NAMES FOR KEMET

The foreign name for Kemet, 'Egypt' is ultimately derived from the name of the Ptah cult centre, Hikaptah. The Greeks have translated it as 'Aigyptos' and in some languages it has been borrowed and evolved into 'Egypt' or something similar. Some of the people of Canaan and elsewhere in the vicinity refer to Egypt as 'Mitzrayim', the 'divided land'.

The principal attraction of Memphis is the giant temple complex dedicated to Ptah. It's called the Hikaptah ('House of the Soul of Ptah') and its perimeter is defined by an impressive mud-brick enclosure wall. On entering the compound, you can't help but notice the colossal stone statues of Ramesses II flanking the temple's great gateway. Ptah is not to be ignored in his own house, however, and there are plenty of his images as well. The entrance portal leads to a pillared hall and courts and chambers beyond. The local guards and priests will let you know how far you may proceed, if at all.

There are a number of shrines for special cults to be found in Memphis but most notable is that of the Apis bull. Like the Mer-wer bull of Iunu, the black Apis bull of Memphis is a living animal that is treated as the manifestation of a god, in this case, the local favourite Ptah. The

Apis bull is identified by very special markings on its hide including a white triangle on its forehead. The sacred bull is given first-class treatment and is ceremonially paraded out from time to time to the awe and delight of onlookers.

The Apis bull is also believed to have oracular powers. When respectfully asked yes/no questions, the bull answers by wandering into one of two stables. 'If only life were that simple!', you may exclaim, but Egyptians take the method seriously and consider the bull's answers authoritative. Like Mer-wer, the Apis bull is given full honours upon its death and is mummified and installed in a nearby tomb alongside his predecessors. Thereafter, the countryside is searched for a new Apis bull and the cycle continues.

A stay in grand old Memphis provides an excellent opportunity to learn about the Egyptian system of government.

THE LIVING BULL

Foreign visitors to Egypt might be perplexed by the living bull cults found in places such as Iunu, Memphis and Akhmim. As a strong and virile animal, the bull is a symbol of power and fertility, a desired trait of divine entities. Several pharaohs, Ramesses II being one of them, include the title 'the strong bull' in their list of names.

Egypt maintains a hierarchical structure of civil and religious bureaucrats from the pharaoh on down. A basic understanding of the system will help you appreciate how Egypt's ability to organize vast numbers of people has produced many of the architectural marvels that you'll encounter as you journey through Memphis and beyond.

PHARAOH ALMIGHTY

STARTING AT THE TOP, WE HAVE the ruler himself, whom the Egyptians consider to be a living visible god. As such, he serves as the ultimate connection between humans on earth and the world of the deities. The divine pedigree of the pharaoh identifies him as the living embodiment of the god Horus, son of the gods Osiris and Isis. He also proclaims himself to be the son of Ra, the sun-god. Whatever you as an outsider might think of such assertions, the fact remains that the pharaoh is perceived and treated as a divine being with appropriate authority over human affairs – including yours while you're in his country. The obligations of the ruler are many. Of paramount importance is his role as the ultimate high priest. In order to maintain national *maat*, the Egyptian notion of truth and justice resulting in cosmic stability, the pharaoh must make sure the gods are happy and cooperative. Temples must be built, maintained, enhanced or restored, and regular offerings must be presented.

NAMES OF THE PHARAOH

In the Egyptian language, the divine ruler is known as the *nesoo*, which means something quite different from the term *wer* ('great one') that can be applied to mere human rulers elsewhere in the world. The term 'pharaoh' is derived from the Egyptian words *per aa*, meaning literally, 'the great house', an expression denoting the office of kingship. The ruler maintains five official names that are a reflection of his divine descent, responsibilities and his distinction as an individual: A 'Horus name', followed by a 'Two Ladies name' (the ladies being the goddesses Nekhbet and Wadjet who represent Upper and Lower Egypt), then a 'Golden Falcon' name, and finally a throne name and birth name, as found written in the elongated oval cartouches. Ramesses II's grandiose full name is:

The strong bull, beloved of Maat; protector of Egypt, who subdues foreign enemies;
rich of years, great of victories; King of Upper and Lower Egypt,
Usermaatre-setepenre – 'The Justice of Ra is Powerful, Chosen of Ra';
Ramesses-meryamun – 'It is Ra that has begotten him, Beloved of Amun'

There's no doubt who rules Egypt. You'll see statues and monuments celebrating Ramesses II at every turn.

The divine ruler, of course, has his secular duties as the 'Lord of the Two Lands'. His word is law and his royal decrees are to be obeyed. He must rule with wisdom and *maat* and you might notice that he is occasionally depicted as a godly shepherd holding in his hands a crook and a flail. The crook is to guide his human flock gently, while the flail is for administering discipline as needed. The pharaoh is also the commander-in-chief of Egypt's formidable armed forces, a job that assists in fulfilling his responsibilities as the protector of the land and its people.

Becoming the pharaoh is typically a matter of birth. The oldest surviving son of the living ruler becomes the next king. There are exceptions, including the rare female pharaoh, such as Hatshepsut a few hundred years ago, or in political situations that trigger a dynastic transition.

ROYAL DYNASTIES

Some 900 years from now, an Egyptian priest by the name of Manetho will organize Egyptian rulers into historical divisions based primarily on ruling lines of kings or 'dynasties'. Although not perfect, the system is quite useful in allowing one to discuss trends, events and people in their proper sequence. However, if you mention the current 19th dynasty to any Egyptians you meet on your journey now, in 1250 BC, they will only stare at you blankly and assume you are an ignorant foreigner.

The rulers of Egypt have not forgotten their royal ancestors. Formal king-lists exist, some carved in stone, which trace the line of kingship back to Menes. Ramesses II, for example, has incised such a list in his new temple at Abdju (Abydos). As you might expect, rulers who are considered illegitimate or disastrous are omitted, in the hope that they will quickly be forgotten. These include a couple of individuals from the last dynasty: the female pharaoh Hatshepsut and the religious heretic Akhenaten.

Seti I, the father of Ramesses II, displays some of the many symbols of kingship, including a royal headdress, an artificial strap-on beard and the sekhem *sceptre, an emblem of power.*

A number of kings have actually served as 'co-regents' alongside their fathers. This is a sensible procedure, providing a hands-on internship in the heavy responsibilities of kingship, as well as a safeguard for stability in the event of assassination, as happened to King Amenemhet I about 700 years ago. However, if the pharaoh's oldest son is bizarre or unstable, as in the case of the religious heretic Amenhotep IV (also known as Akhenaten) about 120 years ago, it can really shake things up (see Chapter VII for the sordid details).

Given the high child mortality rate, the pressure for the pharaoh to produce a viable male heir is significant, and in order to produce royal offspring, the ruler requires fertile consorts. Although the average Egyptian maintains only one wife, and a few high-ranking officials might exceptionally have two or more, the pharaoh can have as many as he wants. Some royal wives have come from the ranks of commoners while others are drawn directly from the upper-class. Foreign wives might be offered to the pharaoh as tribute or to cement political alliances. As appalling as it might seem to the outsider, the regal bloodline has been maintained many times by the king marrying his own sister or half-sister. Occasionally a pharaoh has even married his own daughter, although such marriages are usually only ceremonial and not intended to produce children.

The official transfer of royal power takes place on the death of the ruling pharaoh. According to the Egyptian mythological scenario, the deceased pharaoh takes his place as the god Osiris, ruler of the Netherworld and judge of the dead, while his heir becomes the new living Horus on the throne of Egypt.

Lengths of reign, obviously, have varied significantly over the centuries. Back in the great days of pyramid-building, Pepi II was said to have ruled for as many as ninety-four years, though perhaps to the disadvantage of Egypt as a whole, which fell into civil war not long after his death. On the other hand, tradition recalls that many years ago during a period of political instability, seventy kings ruled in seventy days. This seems unlikely, but the statement does suggest that the royal house must have been in a bit of a mess. Our own Ramesses II is in his seventies; he has ruled competently for fifty-four years thus far, outlived several potential heirs and shows no signs of imminent demise.

The latest line of rulers (19th dynasty) began with Ramesses I, the present king's grandfather. Ramesses wasn't born into the role but was a high-ranking official and a general under King Horemheb, a

CALENDAR

There's no getting away from the centrality of the ruler in Egyptian society – even the civil calendar is based on the years of a pharaoh's reign. A particular date might read: Year 3, season of Shemu, third month, day 4 under the majesty of King So-and-So.

military leader himself and one of a few transitional rulers after 'the Akhenaten fiasco' during the latter part of the 18th dynasty. Horemheb appointed Ramesses I as his successor and the traditional father-to-son succession would be re-established again thereafter. This first Ramesses barely had enough time to enjoy his pharaonic perks before dying in office after less than two years to be replaced by his son, the new living Horus, Seti. Seti had a splendid run of about ten years as pharaoh. His military campaigns took him into Palestine and Syria and his wonderful building accomplishments include the lovely summer palace which formed the core of the new royal city in the Delta, Pi-Ramesses.

RAMESSES THE GREAT HIMSELF

THAT BRINGS US TO THE PRESENT ruler, Ramesses II, whose name, likeness and accomplishments will assail you nearly everywhere you travel in Egypt. As next in line for the throne, young Ramesses II established himself early as a man of action, participating in a number of royal activities with his father and contributing to military campaigns while still a teenager. After inheriting the kingship, Ramesses immediately displayed an insatiable appetite for monumental architecture, completing some of his father's building projects and initiating plenty of his own. In the fourth year of his reign, he began his own bold military campaigns, striking out at Syria to the East. In the following year he fought against the Hittites during the famous battle of Kadesh, which he still can't stop boasting about even fifty years later.

The Hittites, with their capital in Anatolia (Turkey), were likewise building their own aggressive empire in competition with the Egyptians. In the twenty-first year of his reign, Ramesses made an unprecedented peace-treaty with the Hittite king, Hattusilis III. This non-aggression pact was a wise move: it established acceptable spheres of influence and fostered a sense of peaceful coexistence between these two powerful long-time enemies. Without it, it's unlikely that you, as a foreign visitor, would be able to enjoy the relative safety and leisure of an Egyptian visit right now. Several years after the treaty, Ramesses accepted the daughter of Hattusilis as a royal wife, and later took another Hittite bride.

Speaking of brides, Ramesses II has quite a few. His most beloved great royal wives include Nefertari and Isetnofret.

NEFERTARI

Nefertari was Ramesses II's first wife whom he married before he became pharaoh. By all accounts she seems to have been his favourite and was a genuine beauty. At the site of Meha in Nubia (see Chapter IX), he constructed two immense temples built into sandstone mountains. One is dedicated to himself and other gods and the second to Nefertari, a rare and dramatic homage to a royal consort. Her magnificently painted tomb is sadly out of bounds down in Thebes. Despite the similarity in names, don't confuse Nefertari with Nefertiti. Although likewise said to be very beautiful, the latter was the controversial wife of the 'heretic' pharaoh Akhenaten from the previous dynasty.

Sadly, the former died a couple of decades ago, but since then Ramesses has had many other wives to console him, including at least three of his own daughters. Although it's hard to count them all, Ramesses seems to have around fifty sons thus far – and probably just as many daughters – from his various royal wives.

Ramesses II's building accomplishments are, of course, impressive, and above all, numerous. Did you blink? You might have just missed another colossal statue, temple or some other monument dedicated by or to His Majesty. You might hear rumours that quality of construction has suffered to quantity in comparison to, say, the works of his father, Seti. Look around while you're touring Kemet and decide for yourself.

ALL THE KING'S MEN

AS THE DUTIES OF THE PHARAOH of Egypt include nothing less than the maintenance of the entire cosmic universe, the tasks required to keep a society running smoothly are certainly too much for one person to handle – even a living god. The ruler therefore presides over a huge network of bureaucrats who manage the government, economy and military in the earthly sphere, and perform divine services on the pharaoh's behalf in the world of the gods.

At the top of the pharaoh's pyramid of power is the *tjaty*, or 'vizier'. The position is as close to the king as any mere mortal is likely to reach. These days, there are two of them, one to supervise Upper Egypt and another to administer the Delta, and both are among the busiest men in Egypt. They receive reports from the highest bureaucrats in the land and give a daily briefing to the pharaoh – no matter what sort of mood he's in. As a high judge, the vizier also presides over legal proceedings ranging from serious criminal cases to mundane property disputes. Many posts in the Egyptian bureaucracy are traditionally hereditary,

BUREAUCRATS

It's not uncommon for bureaucrats to have more than one title or a whole string of them. The titles of an official named Rekhmire who served during the reigns of Thutmose III and Amenhotep II, for example, included 'Vizier', 'Mayor of the City of Thebes', 'Superintendent of Archives', 'Steward of the Palace', 'Superintendent of the Two Treasuries of Gold and of Silver', 'Administrator of All Works in Karnak', and 'Confidential Controller'. He also boasted a handful of priestly titles and a wide range of complementary epithets such as 'Confidant of the King', 'One Who Fills the Storehouses' and 'Dispenser of Justice Impartially'.

but the paramount job of the vizier requires a direct royal appointment.

Below the vizier are a number of other essential high-ranking officials. The Overseer of Works, for example, deals with the numerous official construction projects such as temples, palaces or monuments. With a big-spending megalomaniacal pharaoh as his present boss, Ramesses's Overseer of Works is kept rather busy at the moment. At the local level are the governors of the many provinces you will

Treasury scribes busily record the iniquities of tax dodgers as a village leader is brought to account.

pass through on your Egyptian adventure. These officials must answer to the vizier, with dismissals and punishment possible consequences for incompetence.

There are so many people in Egypt with one sort of official title or another that it seems that half the population are bureaucrats. You might encounter overseers of horned cattle, beekeepers, sandal-makers and tambourine players. The specialized servants responsible for keeping the king happy and maintaining the day-to-day running of his royal palaces are near-infinite in number and variety, as are the people who manage them. In the lower ranks, there is still a meritocratic ideal that those who excel will rise regardless of their background, although in reality the likelihood of advancing from assistant clerk in a small town to the office of vizier is minimal. Such a lofty goal might be a great motivational dream for young men in scribal schools, but favouritism and upper-class family connections remain strong factors in determining who gets to do what in Egypt.

One of the most powerful bureaucrats in Egypt is the state Treasurer, whose difficult job it is to ensure that Egypt's vast domestic and foreign wealth is collected and distributed. Beneath him serve the Overseer of the Granaries and

AN EDICT

Thievery of property owed to the state, and abuses by official and fraudulent tax collectors were serious problems during the reign of Horemheb a few decades ago. The king addressed this situation with an edict engraved on a large stone stele (tablet) erected in the Karnak temple at Thebes. The stone proclaimed that anyone who took advantage of the common man or the state in such a way could have their nose cut off and be banished to border towns such as Tjaru on the eastern frontier, where they could enviously watch foreigners come and go.

the Overseer of Fields. The former ensures that the massive state granaries are full: as grain is the main commodity of exchange in Egypt, the granaries serve as a kind of central bank from which the numerous bureaucrats and other dependents of the state can be paid. The latter collects taxes from farmlands, whether private or state-owned or leased. Although the king technically owns all of the land in Egypt, in practice ordinary people own, inherit, buy and sell land or receive land-grants from the ruler. Avoiding the payment of property taxes, however, is not an option. Egyptians can expect an annual visit from the official tax assessor who will demand grain, cattle or work duty for the state as payment. Those who don't pay face confiscation of their property or perhaps a little unpleasant government labour that will likely involve moving heavy stones.

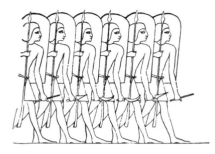

Equipped with the latest weaponry, the army is well-trained and ready for action.

ing extensive – and implausible – mayhem on the enemy). The army is a highly professional organization these days: there are career officers supported by a bureaucracy and many of the troops are rewarded with land-grants, cattle, slaves or a share of foreign booty. Some soldiers, however, are conscripts and there is also a large contingent of foreign troops captured as prisoners of war or recruited from places such as Nubia.

THE MILITARY

EGYPT'S POWER AND WEALTH ARE physically sustained by an advanced military that protects the homeland from foreign incursions and extends the long arm of Kemet's might wherever the pharaoh desires. Egypt maintains a series of frontier forts in the south, west and east to protect against intrusions by the 'vile' and 'wretched' Nubians, Libyans and various Asiatic peoples. The pharaoh himself, typically joined by one of his sons, will often lead the army into battle (usually returning alive and boasting of personally inflict-

THE ARMY

The army as it stands today consists of about 20,000 troops plus accompanying support staff. At its most basic level, fifty men are organized into platoons and five platoons constitute a company. Twenty companies form a division and there are four divisions of 5,000 supervised by generals. These divisions are named after four gods: Ra, Ptah, Amun and Seth.

Horse-drawn chariots are among the most effective and terrifying weapons in the Egyptian arsenal.

Whatever their national origin, Egyptian soldiers are quite adept at marching for long distances over many days, although naval vessels are available for troop transport up and down the Nile and occasionally to places such as the Canaanite coast. Expect to see the army as you travel, especially in the large cities and at the frontiers.

Egyptian soldiers are proficient in the use of a number of weapons. From a distance, the bow and arrow and javelin can be used with devastating effect. Close combat can be especially brutal, with bronze axes, spears, swords and daggers serving as effective slashing and stabbing tools. The average foot soldier doesn't seem to wear much body armour, but shields made of stretched cowhides can provide some protection.

The elite of the Egyptian military are the charioteers. It is the glamour job in the army, if there is such a thing, combining modern technology, speed and the power of galloping horses. The concept of the chariot came from the east

THE MEDJAY

The Medjay are a nomadic tribe of people wandering the eastern deserts of Lower Nubia. For many years, the Egyptians have been effectively drafting or recruiting the often cooperative Medjay as scouts, special military troops and policemen. They have a reputation for being enthusiastic warriors.

WEAPONS

One of the fiercest personal weapons in the Egyptian arsenal is the *khepesh* sword. Its bronze blade is shaped like a sickle or scimitar and is ideally suited for lopping off heads and limbs during the heat of battle. Such sharp weapons certainly prove handy when it comes to counting the enemy dead. Hands and other body parts are often dramatically heaped up in piles to demonstrate the fearsome power of the Egyptian forces. For accounting purposes, one hand per victim provides an accurate assessment of casualties. Throwing both on the heap, though, makes a bigger pile, a larger count and a happier Ramesses.

and the Egyptians have learned to exploit this tool to defeat Eastern enemies such as the Hittites. Fast and manoeuvrable, chariots are to be feared and they are. They're fun to watch but stay out of their way; they are difficult to stop, and being run over by a horse and chariot is probably one of the more painful ways to die in Egypt. And please don't ask for a ride.

The typical chariot unit consists of the driver, a bowman and occasionally a shield-bearer to protect the driver, who requires both hands to steer. Charioteers wear body armour consisting of brass scales sewn onto a leather corset, and occasionally a helmet. (The pharaoh himself is sometimes depicted wearing a blue leather 'war crown' or helmet while firing arrows from his speeding vehicle.) Chariots are very high maintenance, requiring frequent repair of the vehicles and expert care of the horses. If

you arrived in Egypt from the east via the frontier fort of Tjaru and nearby Pi-Ramesses, you may have noticed the stables and weapons factories busy at work for the next military campaign. Were you intimidated? Good – that's the desired effect.

THE MEMPHIS EXPERIENCE

NOW THAT YOU HAVE A GOOD understanding of the power of Egypt's ruler and the complexity of its government, you're ready to appreciate Memphis to the full. Visit the palaces, temples and marketplaces. Contemplate the city's historical significance and savour its regal, cosmopolitan atmosphere and religious ambience. Take in its many unique sights, sounds and (often pungent) scents while the Nile breezes soothingly moderate the noontime heat.

V · MOUNTAINS OF
THE PHARAOHS

Djoser's Landmark ◆ *Khufu's Masterpiece*
Man-lion of the Desert ◆ *Downsizing*
Dealing with the Dead ◆ *Facing Eternity*

TRAVELLING SOUTH FROM Iunu (Heliopolis) towards Men-nefer (Memphis), you cannot help but notice the spectacular range of ivory-coloured mountains off to the west. These are the famous pyramids of Egypt known far and wide as monuments worthy of marvel. They really are quite astonishing and serve as yet another reminder of the Egyptians' capacity for superb engineering, spiritual devotion and organizing large numbers of people. Even in Ramesses' day the pyramids are already quite old; the largest was built around 1,400 years before the time of your visit. A chain of the oldest pyramids stretches north to south for dozens of miles along the fringes of the western desert, a record in stone of a long-vanished era of divine rulers.

The shape of the pyramid is steeped in mythology. It can be seen as a primeval mound from which the creator-god Atum emerged. In this sense, the shape resembles the ancient *benben*-stone honoured in Atum's temple in Iunu. The pyramids also reach towards the sun and thereby form a kind of spiritual stairway for the deceased ruler to ascend to the sky where he can join the sun-god Ra as he voyages across the heavens and descends into the Netherworld.

To track the physical origins of the pyramids, we need to look back to the beginnings of the Egyptian state around 2,000 years ago. The earliest rulers were buried mostly at the southern site of Abdju (Abydos), which you'll encounter if you choose to continue your journey south to Waset (Thebes). The visible parts of their tombs are large rectangular mud-brick structures with mounds of sand on top; the burial itself is concealed in an underground chamber carved into the bedrock. These relatively simple structures were built for a few centuries with occasional variations. During the 3rd dynasty, however, a king by the name of Djoser initiated a revolutionary burial complex at Saqqara that set the trend for future tombs.

DJOSER'S LANDMARK

SAQQARA IS PART OF THE VAST royal and elite necropolis of Memphis that stretches for dozens of miles north and south of the great city along the western desert. Probably named after a favourite funerary god of Memphis, Sokar, it has been in continuous use as a cemetery since Egypt was initially unified. The area is home to eleven royal pyramids along with several small subsidiary 'queen's pyramids' and hundreds

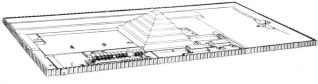

Djoser's step-pyramid complex at Saqqara is a sprawling memorial in stone.

of tombs of high-placed bureaucrats. Although Egypt's rulers no longer choose to be buried there, tombs of the elite continue to be constructed in the vicinity.

Djoser's innovation at Saqqara was this: rather than settling for the usual rectangular tomb, he enlarged his burial monument by stacking six such structures one atop the other to form a step pyramid. Mud-brick was replaced with stone and the resulting configuration was something that had never before been seen, and probably the largest stone structure in the world at the time. It stands nearly 200 feet tall and, viewed from Memphis, majestically dominates the western skyline. To explore this amazing monument, just walk west from Memphis and ascend to the sandy windblown plateau. The transition will be stark as you proceed from a noisy, bustling metropolis to an equally vast but silent city of the dead. Once on top of the plateau you'll be greeted by the sight of a truly astounding number of tombs and shadowy distant pyramids stretching to both the north and south.

While the step pyramid is startling, it is just part of Djoser's amazing complex of funerary structures associated with his burial, which covers 37 acres and includes many dummy buildings, that is,

structures in stone that imitate bureaucratic and other real-world facilities, built to last an eternity and serve Djoser's administrative needs in the afterlife. There is even a vast plaza on which the spirit of the king can perform the sed-festival until the end of time. (This might have been especially satisfying to Djoser as he only survived seventeen years of reign and thus never achieved the traditional thirty-year anniversary for the renewal ceremonies.)

Apart from the pyramid itself, perhaps the most impressive feature of the whole place is the massive stone wall surrounding the entire complex. Made of limestone, and decorated with hand-carved recessed panels, its entire length extends 5,397 feet and seems to replicate a palace façade. Walk completely around it and see for yourself. There are fourteen gates carved into the wall but only the one on the south-east corner is real, providing access into the compound.

Djoser's pyramid complex is ancient and essentially abandoned. If you convince those who might guard the place – if any can still be found – to allow you to have a stroll around inside its walls, you will be awed by its impressive scale and exemplary stonework. Should you make your way around to the north side

ARCHITECTURAL GENIUS

The architect given credit for the design of Djoser's innovative funerary compound was a high priest of Iunu named Imhotep. To this day, many centuries later, he remains venerated as an architectural genius and as a patron of scribes and physicians. In the future, he will actually be deified and worshipped in temples built to his honour.

of the pyramid, you will find a small stone building with a couple of holes at about eye level. Take a look inside and prepare to be startled: Djoser himself will stare back at you! As your heart rate returns to normal, you'll realize that it's only a realistic seated statue of the pharaoh. The holes in the wall aren't for you to look in; they're to allow Djoser to look out and see the world.

KHUFU'S MASTERPIECE

THE NEXT LINE OF RULERS (4th dynasty) took pyramid building to its apogee. If you look south across the desert from Saqqara, you can see some of their earlier construction 'experiments' in the distance, especially those of the king Sneferu. To see one of the greatest pyramid-building achievements in history, however, you absolutely must hire a boat and make a downstream sojourn about 14 miles north of Mem-

phis to another part of the city's vast necropolis, Giza, where you will find the pyramid of Sneferu's son, Khufu. Named 'The Horizon of Khufu', its now slightly sun-varnished exterior must have once gleamed stunningly bright in the relentless Egyptian sun. There are numerous impressive monuments to be found up and down the Nile, but the size, beauty and precision of this pyramid's architecture remains unsurpassed.

Like Saqqara, much of the Giza site is now more or less abandoned. You might be approached by individuals offering to be your guide but take any information they tell you with a grain of salt. Given that Khufu's pyramid is over 1,400 years old, there are probably few who can still give accurate details on how it was all done, although that certainly won't stop some from trying.

Perhaps as amazing as the pyramid itself are the technical requirements needed to accomplish such a project. Some 20,000–30,000 men might have been required to finish the job during Khufu's lifetime and construction probably took about twenty-five years. The quarrying alone was a mammoth task, even with much of the stone being obtained directly from the limestone plateau on which the pyramid sits. There's a source of fine limestone across the river and granite said to have been used in the interior came from as far south as Sunu (Aswan) at Egypt's southern border, 600 miles away.

Using systems of ramps and levers to move and lift stones, well-organized

Khufu's Great Pyramid on the Giza plateau, although abandoned, is a magnificent testament to human ingenuity.

teams required lots of brute strength and coordinated timing to shift the heavy blocks into place as the pyramid grew. Apart from the stonecutters and draggers, there must have been a huge number of support staff to provide bread, beer, medical attention and other services for the workers. An on-site town was required to house everyone involved in the project. Access to the Nile by canal and an artificial harbour brought men, building materials and other supplies close to the building site. The king, too, as the ultimate overseer of the construction, had a palace in the vicinity. As you look around the Giza plateau, you will find few traces of the once industrious community that supported the construction of these incredible monuments.

Of course, Khufu's pyramid is more than just a pile of rocks. There are said

HERE ARE A FEW FACTS ABOUT KHUFU'S GREAT PYRAMID

Its four faces are precisely oriented to the four cardinal directions and are pitched at a steady angle of approximately 51 degrees.

♦♦♦

The pyramid's base dimensions are 756 feet on each side, covering an area of approximately 13 square acres.

♦♦♦

A rough estimate of the number of stones constituting the structure approaches 2,300,000, if not many more.

♦♦♦

The pyramid stands an astonishing 481 feet tall. In fact, it's the tallest building on earth and will remain so for another 2,500 years.

HERODOTUS

About 750 years from now, the Greek historian Herodotus will visit Egypt and
record some of the tales he hears about the building of the great pyramid by
Khufu (whom he refers to as 'Cheops'). According to Herodotus, Cheops was a
nasty fellow who 'brought the people to utter misery', forcing them to work on
his pyramid over a period of thirty years. Fed on a diet of garlic, onions and
radishes, claims Herodotus, it took the unwilling workers ten years just to build
the road on which the stones were dragged. Building a pyramid is an expensive
proposition and Herodotus tells us that 'so evil a man was Cheops that he made
his own daughter to sit in a chamber and exact payment' as a prostitute in order
to fund the project. The latter story is so farfetched that it's likely that
Herodotus' informant was a descendant of one of the 'free-lance historians'
you'll find lurking about Giza in search of gullible tourists.

to be several interior passages and chambers, no doubt just as grand, that serve as the burial place of the god-king. And as is common with many of Egypt's pyramids, the pyramid itself does not stand alone, but is accompanied by a complex of related structures. A small temple for the perpetuation of priestly offerings stands on its eastern side and is connected by a causeway to a funerary 'valley temple' situated on the Nile.

Also on the pyramid's eastern side are three small pyramids belonging to Khufu's mother and two of his queens. Nearby to the west and east are rows of tombs belonging to officials of the realm, their rectangular stone superstructures resembling blocks aligned in streets. The deceased are interred in crypts below, but above ground are chapels where devoted visitors can present offerings in front of a false door carved in stone. The door, it is believed,

allows the soul of the deceased to pass from the land of the dead to that of the living. Should the physical offerings cease, the walls of these chapels are splendidly carved with scenes of all that might be desired in the present life and the hereafter. These kinds of tombs are plentiful and can be found around nearly any pyramid complex, but few, if any, are still maintained. A respectful visit to such chapels will reward one with a glimpse of a much older Egypt whose culture was in many ways just as sophisticated as it is now in the reign of Ramesses II. Stroll through the maze of these tombs but don't worry about getting lost; the imposing hulk of Khufu's pyramid will keep you oriented.

Close by Khufu's pyramid is that of his son, Khafre. It's almost as impressive as his father's and at first glance might appear even taller, although this is an optical illusion due to its being built on

slightly higher ground. The pyramid's name, 'Khafre is the Greatest', implies a competition between father and son for the largest burial monument. Give it a walk-around and admire its size and beauty and decide the winner for yourself. When you reach its southern side, wander on over to the third major pyramid in the group, that of Khafre's son, Menkaure. In comparison to its colossal neighbours, it appears quite diminutive, but this little beauty of a pyramid is accented by over a dozen rows of exterior casing blocks carved from red granite imported from the southern quarries hundreds of miles to the south.

Now for the sad part. With all that time and effort expended on these magnificent pyramids, they were utter failures: not one of them was effective in

Khufu's son Khafre built his own imposing pyramid next to his father's. It looks bigger because it's cleverly built on higher ground.

TOMB RAIDERS

Robbing the pyramids must have been a tremendous effort. Entrance tunnels were blocked with huge blocks of stone designed to frustrate – and possibly crush – any would-be thief. But the power of human greed is strong, and ultimately even these deterrents failed.

As you walk around Giza, you might notice the pyramids' once sealed and hidden entrances visible on their north faces, where the blocks have been dislodged by tomb raiders.

protecting the interred rulers from robbery and probably physical destruction. When you visit the old pyramids and their accompanying cemeteries, you are basically visiting the abandoned ruins of a time long ago. The priests no longer perform the daily rites for the likes of Sneferu, Khufu, or any of the others. In fact, following the civil war, stones from the pyramid temples and causeways were already being pilfered by other pharaohs to enhance their own burial structures. Perhaps they maintained the attitude that the property of one living Horus belonged to the next. Ramesses II won't be buried in a pyramid. He and all of his predecessors since the expulsion of the Hyksos are all buried in a 'secret' cemetery near Thebes.

MAN-LION OF THE DESERT

APART FROM THE PYRAMIDS, one of the greatest attractions in the region is the great sphinx of Khafre. This truly enormous sculpture is situated downhill below the pyramids of Khufu and Khafre, close to the latter's valley temple. The sphinx merges the body of a recumbent lion with the head of the pharaoh, combining the brute strength of nature's strongest animal with the intelligence and wisdom of humanity. The head of the statue was carved from a protruding outcrop of limestone and its body was excavated from the surrounding rock. When this part of the necropolis of Memphis was eventually abandoned, it was only a matter of time

Half god-king and half lion, the Great Sphinx at Giza evokes the power of Egypt's rulers.

before this wondrous monument was buried up to its neck in sand.

The sphinx, however, experienced a revival during the last dynasty of rulers (18th dynasty). If you look between his paws, you'll notice a large inscribed stele. Its text tells the story of a young prince on a desert hunting expedition who took a nap near the buried sphinx's head and experienced a prophetic dream: if the ruler would dig the great monument out of the sand and restore its sanctity, he would become ruler of Egypt. In the words of the sphinx's inscription:

You shall be for me a protector...the sand of the desert upon which I am has reached me; turn to me, to have that done which I have desired, knowing that you are my son, my protector; come here, behold, I am with you, I am your leader.

SPECIAL INTEREST

The eldest living son of Ramesses II, Khaemwaset, has taken a special interest in the past, clearing away debris and identifying the monuments of his royal ancestors in the cemeteries of Memphis and elsewhere. As the high-priest of Ptah, he is in charge of the Apis bull cult and has built an underground catacomb at Saqqara to house the bulls' remains. If he manages to outlive his father, perhaps he will be the next ruler of Upper and Lower Egypt.
(Note: he didn't.)

The sand was cleared away and when his father, the great Amenhotep II, passed on to the great beyond, the young prince became the new ruler of Egypt: Thutmose IV. The sphinx is now worshipped as Horemakhet, a manifestation of the sun, and a temple for his worship continues to be maintained by Ramesses II.

DOWNSIZING

It's easy to see why massive building projects such as that of Khufu proved just as exhausting to the economy as to the stone-draggers. The building of massive pyramids peaked during the 4th dynasty with the likes of Sneferu, Khufu and Khafre. Thereafter, even with the pyramid of Khafre's son Menkaure, a dramatic decrease in the size of the monuments became a pat-tern. With the site of Giza seemingly taken up with the truly great pyramids, the 5th-dynasty rulers moved south to another building site before eventually returning to Saqqara. Should you revisit Saqqara after viewing the magnificent stone giants of Giza, the downsizing trend will be obvious. In the vicinity of Djoser's great step-pyramid complex are three diminutive monuments, the 5th- and 6th-dynasty pyramids of the rulers Userkaf, Unis and Teti. In comparison to their gargantuan predecessors they appear as mere lumps on the sandy landscape.

The last pyramid built at Saqqara was that of Pepi II, the long-lived final ruler of the 6th dynasty. Thereafter, Egypt suffered its civil war lasting about 130 years, during which the burials for the various pretenders to the throne were at best weak efforts. Even after Egypt was reunified, pyramids never reached the size and quality of the three at Giza.

As you walk through these fields of famous and impressive monuments, which the desert is slowly but surely reclaiming, try to imagine what they were like in the prime of their day: shining, dignified and revered. And while at Saqqara or Giza, visit a few of the empty tomb chapels of the nobles in their stone rectangular tombs, if any are accessible. There on the walls you will see depictions of Egyptian life as it once was, and in many ways still is, although the relatives have stopped appearing on feast days to have a meal with their beloved.

A fancy coffin, a beautiful shrine, and host of weeping professional mourners send off a wealthy Egyptian in style.

DEALING WITH THE DEAD

AFTER VISITING THE VAST cemeteries of Saqqara and Giza, you can't help but be impressed by the attention given to death in Egypt. This concern not only applies to the rulers with their grandiose monuments and burial chambers, but to ordinary Egyptians as well. Life isn't considered over once the body stops functioning and a lot of care and expense is lavished on the dead. To understand what an outsider might consider to be very bizarre behaviour, one needs to be aware of the belief system that sustains it. The Egyptians do not believe that you have merely a body, or perhaps a body and soul. One's physical being is accompanied by spiritual

SPIRIT-ENTITY

The personal spirit-entity known as the *ba* is often depicted as a bird with a human head. The *ba* is believed to be able to leave the tomb and circulate in the living world before returning back to the body of the deceased. Some Egyptians will interpret migratory birds as *ba*s in transit.

entities that are recognized as vital components of the individual. The *ka* is considered to be one's life essence and is a kind of spirit double. The *ba* might be viewed as one's personality that also inhabits the body. Additionally, one's shadow and name are considered important parts of the Egyptian's being.

When the body dies, the Egyptians believe that the spirit-components of the deceased survive. Mummification attempts to ensure that the *ka* and *ba* still have a physical home. The tomb provides a residence for these elements and serves as an interface between the worlds of the living and the dead. In the process of mummification, the dead person is also transformed into a god, going through the same process that Osiris did when he was resurrected.

Tombs will obviously vary depending on the resources available to a particular individual. For the majority of Egyptians who live their tedious lives as labourers, the 'tomb' might consist of a hole in the ground in the desert outskirts, the body being rolled into a mat and buried with a few handy or cherished possessions: perhaps a comb and a mirror for personal grooming and a jug of beer and some bread for suste-

WHAT A WASTE!

When hearing of the valuable items buried with dead Egyptians, an outsider is likely to exclaim 'What a waste!' Foreigners aren't the only ones to hold this opinion and tomb robbery is quite a problem. Don't be tempted to 'borrow' any grave goods to 'show the folks back home' – penalties for such offences are harsh and suspects' confessions can be extracted by beating the bottoms of their feet and twisting their limbs. Punishments include mutilation, hard labour, or in the case of royal or high-status thievery, death by impalement. For successful thieves, however, the plundering of a royal tomb can mean a big payoff in 'recyclable' goods, including gold, silver, precious stones and high-quality linen and oils.

nance. These provisions are to maintain the *ka* in the hereafter, a place much like the present without as much pain. Wealthier individuals might spend years working on a tomb with a chapel above and a burial chamber below. The chapel's walls can be painted with scenes of an anticipated good afterlife accompanied by symbolic *ka*-pleasing offerings. A beautiful coffin and a variety of comfortable necessities can be interred in the burial chamber. Especially useful are *shabtis*, little servant figurines that are placed in the tomb to do the bidding of the deceased.

The art of preserving a body to last for eternity requires years of practice and a strong stomach. Various levels of mummification are available, depending on what one can afford. The average dead Egyptian thrown in a hole in the desert – the budget option – has it relatively easy. With luck, his body might be somewhat preserved by natural desiccation in dry earth or sand. An artificial mummification, however, is carried out by skilled embalmers adept in turning a decaying corpse into something that more or less resembles a living being.

The tourist with a morbid fascination for such enterprises can attempt to visit an embalmer's workshop. Don't expect any of the locals to volunteer to accompany you; embalmers engage in an essential profession but are generally shunned by the public. Expect the workshop to be crowded with several corpses 'in progress'. You will probably see a stone slab or two with drainage outlets for the initial preparation of the deceased, with numerous large white jars filled with natron standing nearby. Some tables will bear eviscerated bodies covered with the dehydrating agent; look under the table to see the jars containing their internal organs. The fancier tables are used for wrapping. You may see a priest wearing a mask representing Anubis, the god of embalming, as he recites spells over the completed mummy. If you're lucky, you might even be able to inspect a freshly constructed ornate coffin before its new owner leaves the premises.

Most artificial mummification involves some sort of evisceration and drying. The brain can be removed by tools inserted through the nostrils, and a small slit in the abdomen provides entry into the body cavity for the removal of internal organs. The heart, which is considered to be the seat of intelligence and emotion, is usually left inside. The rest of the organs are set aside and preserved in jars, each with a lid portraying a specific protective deity, and later placed in the tomb with the mummy. After gutting, the entire body is treated for perhaps two months with natron, a naturally dehydrating mineral compound mostly derived from an ancient dry lake bed in the north-western desert.

There are other procedures to ensure that the body 'looks good', including packing the nose with linen and rubbing the skin with oils. If all goes well, the *ka* of the deceased will have a recognizable home that more or less resembles what it was used to. The body is typically wrapped in linen, sometimes decorated with jewelry and amulets, and placed in a coffin. With the tomb prepared, a funeral ceremony can ensue.

The sending-off of an affluent or prestigious individual often features a parade of sorts, including a hired contingent of professional wailing women. The eerie sound of these 'mourners' can be disturbing to the tourist but it's also your signal to view the unique spectacle from a distance, or perhaps even close-

NEGATIVE CONFESSION

Wealthier Egyptians can purchase a papyrus scroll containing the information necessary to survive the journey through the Netherworld. Among its many chapters, this *Book of the Dead* provides the proper responses to satisfy the various tribunal gods. Here's a sample from the 'Negative Confession', in which the deceased denies having taken part in any number of illicit activities:

I have not slain a bull which was the property of the god.

♦♦♦

I have not set my mouth in motion [slandered].

♦♦♦

I have not debauched the wife of a man.

♦♦♦

I have not snatched away the bread of the child, nor treated with contempt the god of my city.

♦♦♦

I have terrorized no man.

♦♦♦

I have not multiplied my speech overmuch.

♦♦♦

I have not acted with insufferable insolence.

♦♦♦

I have not purloined offerings.

♦♦♦

I have not committed robbery with violence.

♦♦♦

I have not stolen cultivated land.

♦♦♦

I have not pried into matters.

up as an anonymous member of the procession. The coffin is carried or dragged on a sledge to the tomb chapel where a *sem*-priest conducts the rituals, perhaps in the company of a lector

The Devourer watches hungrily as the heart of the deceased is weighed. For those who can afford it, a copy of the Book of the Dead *provides the clues necessary to survive Judgment and win a happy life in the Afterworld.*

priest. The climax of the service is the 'opening of the mouth', during which the mummy is ceremoniously reanimated. When all is done, the coffin is placed with the funerary provisions in the burial chamber and the room is sealed. Ideally relatives will appear on regular occasions to provide offerings at the chapel; if not, the physical and symbolic provisions will have to suffice. If all goes well, the deceased will become an *akh*, an effective and capable spirit.

FACING ETERNITY

BEING DEAD, PRESERVED AND outfitted with thousands of deben worth of kit is not alone sufficient to guarantee one's passage to eternity. The Egyptians believe in a judgment in which each person's life is assessed for its worthiness to continue in the Netherworld. After death, the spirit of the deceased must first traverse the scary waters and caverns below the earth, where pitfalls and tricksters abound. Wealthier Egyptians are therefore buried with a papyrus

scroll containing instructions for successfully navigating through the obstacles.

With luck – and a reliable travel guide – the spirit eventually arrives at a judgment hall presided over by Osiris, king of the dead. An interrogation takes place and appropriate vindicating answers are expected. The scribal god Thoth takes notes on the proceedings. Ultimately, the deceased's heart is place on the pan of a scale and balanced against the feather of *maat*, representing truth. The scale had better balance or a nasty composite creature called Ammut, 'The Devourer', who has the head of a crocodile, the foreparts of a lion and the hindquarters of a hippo, will consume the wretched soul into non-existence.

On that cheery note, you're now much better equipped to appreciate the cemeteries you'll be encountering as you continue to travel up the Nile. And each evening as the sun sets beautifully into the west, the land of the dead, you'll be able to relate to the Egyptian notion of death like a native and anticipate the sun's 'rebirth' in the morning.

VI · MEET THE PEOPLE

Egyptian Homes • Family Life • Education
Love and Marriage • Working for a Living
Fun and Games

ONCE YOU'VE BEEN SEDUCED BY the grandeur of Egypt's monuments it is easy to get the impression that life in Egypt revolves around the pharaoh and his minions. As a visitor, you may already feel a bit left out of the action; at best, you might view His Majesty from a distance at a festival or as he tours the land with his royal entourage. But in order to really get to know Egypt you need to meet some ordinary Egyptians. Stay in their homes, if they'll let you, tour their villages and fields, and see how they live from day to day. It might prove to be one of the best parts of your trip. In preparation, it may be helpful consider some of the following insights into everyday life and culture as most Egyptians experience it.

EGYPTIAN HOMES

AS YOU JOURNEY DOWN THE Nile, you will see various types of Egyptian dwellings, some built singly among the fields and estates, others clustered in villages and towns. In many villages the houses stand close together, perhaps uncomfortably so, and are arranged in rows separated by narrow streets and alleys. On the river, keep a lookout for the crude herdsmen's huts along the marshes, which are occupied and abandoned throughout the season as needed.

The average working family usually lives in a small house with mud-brick walls and a flat timbered roof. Despite their simplicity, the materials used in mud-brick home construction are very effective in sheltering occupants from the extremes of the Egyptian climate, retaining heat during the winter while remaining cool during the hot summer months. If you're invited to enter one of these houses, keep your elbows tucked in and expect it to be crowded. The interior space can be as small as 10 feet by 25 feet, which includes a living room as well as storage and sleeping rooms. If you look outside into the little back courtyard, you'll see women cooking and washing away from the crush inside. Clearly there's not much privacy with

Egyptian villages are full of small, closely packed homes. Privacy is scarce and visitors will attract a great deal of attention.

The estates of wealthy Egyptians are elaborate affairs featuring large, luxurious homes surrounded by gardens and pools, which require dedicated staff to maintain.

made to look spectacular with the addition of painted plastered walls, floor mosaics and other luxurious features.

Don't pass up the chance to visit an ordinary villager's house or, even better, a nobleman's villa. A moderately well-educated upper class family may well find your foreign ways interesting, if not exotic, for at least a day or two. Your hosts will certainly be pleased to see you if you come bearing a few gifts. You shouldn't expect luxurious accommodation; consider it excellent hospitality if you end up sleeping on a mat on the floor. But don't overstay your welcome: after a day or two the whole village will be observing your every action and talking excitedly about the stranger in their midst.

whole families and neighbours living in such tight quarters. Those with rank and title are able to afford a bit more space. Many live in two-storey villas with gardens full of fruit-bearing trees and sometimes even a landscaped pool. The household servants usually live nearby or on the property of their master.

Royal palaces are in a category all to themselves. Although no expense is spared to bring beauty and comfort to the life of the pharaoh, you might be surprised to know that many of these royal residences are also constructed of mudbrick, just like workers' homes, with wooden ceilings supported by pillars. The architects and craftsmen of Egypt, however, are quite talented and these elaborate mud-built palaces can be

PILLOWS

An ordinary poor Egyptian usually sleeps on a straw mat on the living-room floor, while a nobleman rests on a four-legged bed with a woven platform. As a foreign tourist, you will probably find the Egyptian 'pillow' somewhat curious. A notched block of wood or an artistically rendered wooden, stone or even ivory headrest provides an elevated – and very firm– place to rest one's head during sleep. Pillow fights, needless to say, are not recommended.

FAMILY LIFE

WHEN YOU ENTER A SIMPLE mud-brick Egyptian home, you may notice a number of amulets and images of gods and goddesses who protect the household. These images can be startling to those who aren't accustomed to them. For the Egyptians, however, they are comforting and friendly presences, so don't make jokes about their

The goddess Taweret isn't pretty, but she knows how to protect a pregnant woman.

outlandish appearance. Hekat, for example, takes the form of a frog and oversees childbirth. Taweret is thought to protect a woman during pregnancy and nursing. She has the head and body of a hippo, a crocodile's tail, the hands and feet of a lion, a pregnant belly and pendulous breasts. Bes, perhaps the most frightening of the three, resembles an angry dwarf with a lionesque face; she is typically depicted sporting a feathered headdress and sticking out her tongue. Bes protects children throughout infancy and her image is often found

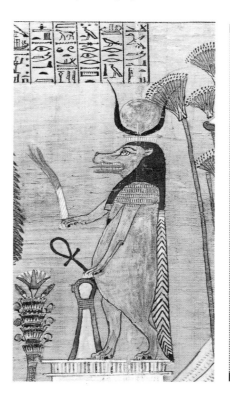

NAMING

The name of an Egyptian is considered a vital part of his being that exceeds the practical need for identification. It becomes part of an individual's eternal existence; without a name, one essentially disappears after death. The Egyptians use the phrase 'to cause one's name to live' to affirm this belief in perpetuating the deceased's memory. By this standard, the pharaohs' proclivity for building monuments with their names carved everywhere certainly advances their long-term survival. Conversely, the destruction of the name of a despised predecessor (such as Hatshepsut and Akhenaten – see Chapters VII and VIII) from their monuments serves the opposite purpose.

Egyptian toys might seem puzzling to outsiders, but the local children certainly love them.

your attempt to fit in, at least they'll be amused by the sunburnt foreigner wearing a linen kilt backwards and calling himself 'Neferhotep'.

As is the case everywhere, play is an important part of growing up in Egypt and the children you meet will probably expect you to show interest in their games and toys. Girls often play with flat, homely, paddle-shaped dolls, while boys enjoy games with sticks and balls. Many children have pets, with dogs, cats and birds among their favourites.

engraved on objects of daily use in the home to drive away demons and other supernatural threats.

Naming a baby is of utmost importance and the parents choose carefully. Names can be descriptive: Nofret, meaning 'beautiful one', is a lovely name for a girl while Nahkt, meaning 'strong', might be applied to a little boy. Panehsy, 'the Nubian', might reflect the baby's dark looks or his actual heritage. Personal names are very often created in combination with that of a god. Amunnakht, for example, means 'the god Amun is strong' and Amunhotep can be translated as 'the god Amun is gracious'. Amun- or Amenhotep is also the name of several previous pharaohs, another reason for its present popularity. Some children acquire pet names, for example, Sitra ('Daughter of Ra'), known as In ('fish'). Try adopting an Egyptian name for yourself while travelling. If the people you meet aren't fooled by

EDUCATION

FOR THE AVERAGE WORKING-class Egyptian, education consists simply of watching and learning from one's parents. A boy accompanies his father to the fields or the workshop and a girl assists her mother in the many tasks of running a household. Formal education, however, is usually reserved for the male children of the upper classes who attend school in preparation for serving in the state bureaucracy. Occasionally a few students are recruited from the humbler classes and some of the girls from noble families learn to read and write from private tutors, but by and large the system is overwhelmingly elitist and only a small fraction of the population is literate.

The Egyptian school curriculum is centred around written language, proper speech and mathematics. Mathematics is an especially important subject, given all the accounting, land measurement and construction matters that Egyptian bureaucrats have to deal with. Some students might also study foreign languages such as Canaanite, Phoenician or Babylonian (Akkadian). Much of the learning takes place by reading, reciting and copying classic texts that have been chosen to instil a sense of duty and justice in the future professional. After several years of training, the new proto-bureaucrat is ready for apprenticeship and integration into the system.

Should you visit a school, you'll notice the students sitting on the floor in front of their teacher, practising writing on scraps of old broken pottery or flakes of white limestone. The students learn the cursive script first – the one used for everyday documents – and the formal hieroglyphic script second. Discipline is strictly maintained and an inattentive pupil is likely to receive a beating – don't intervene!

LOVE AND MARRIAGE

DESPITE ITS ROMANTIC SCENERY, the Nile is not a promising place for a holiday fling: you won't meet many unattached adults on your travels. Egyptian society expects that every male will marry and create a family. A member of the working class might take a wife while still in his teens, someone of higher status perhaps waiting a bit later until his education or professional training is complete. Girls often marry between the ages of twelve and fourteen. Egyptians don't view marriage solely as a social

duty: they also appreciate the romance and drama of courtship, as these excepts from a love poem demonstrate:

From a young lady:
My heart flutters hastily,
When I think of my love of you;
It lets me not act sensibly,
It leaps from its place.
It lets me not put on a dress,
Nor wrap my scarf around me;
…Let not the people say of me:
'A woman fallen through love!'
Be steady when you think of him,
My heart, do not flutter!

From a young man:
My sister has come, my heart exults,
My arms spread out to embrace her;
My heart bounds in its place,
Like the red fish in its pond.
O night, be mine forever,
Now that my queen has come!

By the way, don't be shocked if you hear lovers refer to each other as 'brother' or 'sister' – this is just a poetic figure of speech and doesn't imply an actual familial relationship. Cousins and step-siblings are considered acceptable marriage partners, but unions involving a direct blood-link are usually only practised by the royal family. As for multiple spouses, the average Egyptian maintains, and can only afford, one wife at a time, but there is theoretically no limit for the ruler.

The agreement to set up a household is made by consent of a couple with the

ADVICE

Any, a scribe in the palace of the
late Queen Nefertari, offers
the following advice to young men
regarding marriage:

Take a wife while you're young,
That she should make a son for you;
She should bear for you while you're
youthful,
It is proper to make people.

Happy the man whose people are many,
He is saluted on account of his progeny.

approval of the parents. Either member
of the married couple may initiate
divorce, although there can be serious
financial consequences for doing this.

As for your own amorous pursuits, be
discreet and on your best behaviour
while in Egypt. Adultery with a married
woman is considered a serious breach of
morality and public decorum and a vio-
lation of the religious code of conduct,
and it can lead to both legal and personal
reprisals. Both prostitution and homo-
sexuality are generally frowned upon
and if either appeals to you, it's probably
best not to advertise the fact, especially
as a foreigner.

While the common man typically goes
about his work outside the home,
women serve as household managers,
rearing children, grinding grain and
making bread. Although this might seem
like a form of domestic enslavement, the
women of Egypt actually have a good
deal of power. They can, for example,

own and control property, be witnesses
in court and bring lawsuits, enter into
contracts, or receive and pass on inheri-
tance. Ignore their influence as wives,
mothers and daughters at your own
peril. It is true that women aren't found
in most professional and official occupa-
tions, although some occupy positions as
'singer' or 'chantress' in a temple.

WORKING FOR A LIVING

AS YOU PLACIDLY SAIL UP, OR
drift down, the Nile, viewing the
endless fields of grain and flax, an outsider might get the impression that
something here is delightfully different
and more special than life back home.
Yet, as much as you might fantasize
about an idyllic rural existence in Egypt,
for the majority of the population, producing the Black Land's bounty involves
constant hard physical labour. Apart
from the necessary tasks of hoeing,
planting, harvesting and so forth, the
maintenance of irrigation canals and the
watering of fields seem never-ending.

A good many other jobs in Egypt are,
in fact, rather tough and unpleasant. In
a classic work of literature copied over
and over by Egyptian students, the woes
of the working man are explicitly
described in contrast to the comfortable
life of the professional classes:

I have seen a coppersmith at his work at the
door of his furnace. His fingers were like
the claws of a crocodile, and he stank more
than fish excrement...The reed-cutter goes

The life of an Egyptian nobleman and his family is far more comfortable and pleasant than it is for those who diligently work his land.

downstream to the Delta to fetch himself arrows...When the gnats sting him and the sand fleas bite him as well, then he is judged.

CORVÉE LABOUR

The Egyptian worker lives with the constant threat that he will be yanked away from his job and compelled to work on government projects. This system of corvée labour is often justified as a form of taxation. It provides the large-scale of manpower required for building the latest temple or other royal project. These are not career-building job placements: typical tasks for government draftees might include dragging large blocks of stone.

The potter is covered with earth, although his lifetime is still among the living. He burrows in the field more than swine to bake his cooking vessels...I shall also describe to you the bricklayer. What he experiences is painful. When he must be outside in the wind, he lays bricks without a garment... His strength has vanished through fatigue and stiffness...He eats bread with his fingers, although he washes himself but once a day...The washerman launders at the riverbank in the vicinity of the crocodile...he weeps when he spends all day with a beating stick and a stone there.

The ultimate purpose of this exaggerated description of working-class misery is to convince the student to stay in school and learn the scribal arts, ensuring him a successful and comfortable future.

VIII *The goddess Isis and her dead husband, Osiris, are wonderfully proud of their hawk-headed son, Horus, whom the living pharaoh embodies.*

IX With its stunning pylons, obelisks and courtyards, the temple of Karnak at Thebes offers
perpetual tribute to the god Amun-Ra.

ABOVE: X At the root of Egypt's prosperity are millions of hard-working farmers who till, plant and harvest the fields nourished by the Nile.

FOLLOWING PAGES: XI Far from the eyes of most Egyptians (and probably most tourists), one of Ramesses' greatest constructions is a spectacular temple honouring himself and the gods at Meha, deep in Nubia.

XII *Had she not been erased from history, Hatshepsut's memorial temple would be maintained by a loyal team of priests. Though abandoned, it remains a unique architectural achievement.*

Egyptian society benefits from its broad variety of craft specialists. The workers here are involved in the hot, tedious process of melting and casting metal.

As you travel through the country, you will be impressed by the skill of these scorned manual workers and artisans, from carpenters, basketmakers and metalworkers to boatbuilders, beekeepers and winemakers. In nearly any community, for example, you can watch in amazement as finished lengths of rope appear from the hands of a man rubbing bundles of grass or palm fibres between his hands, or observe a potter spinning out vessels of impressive uniformity. These jobs tend to be in the hands of men, but weavers and textile makers are usually women. Really skilled artisans, such as the sculptors, jewellers, specialist furniture-makers and tomb-painters, have a higher status and will usually be employed by the pharaoh and the nobility.

Although technically everyone in Egypt is enslaved to the divine ruler, you will also notice that there are actual slaves in the realm, who are treated as property and can be bought and sold. Many are prisoners of war captured during Egypt's various foreign incursions. They can be given by the state to institutions such as palace or temples, or to individuals.

FUN AND GAMES

EGYPTIANS KNOW HOW TO RELAX and entertain themselves – and the occasional visitor too. Wrestling and stick-fighting are cheap and cheerful pastimes in the villages. A trip with the family for bird-hunting and spearfishing in the marshes can likewise be enjoyable. Visitors take note: you will probably fail to catch so much as a tadpole, but the locals will be entertained by your ineptitude and impressed by your willingness to try.

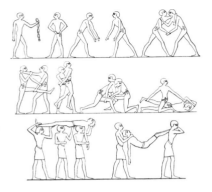

Wrestling, anyone? Or would you prefer to amuse yourself by fighting with sticks and losing?

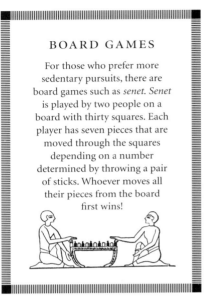
Certain sports are reserved for the elite. Bow-hunting for lions, leopards and wild bulls is a favourite pastime of pharaohs and their companions, as is harpooning hippos. Although the performance is carefully stage-managed to ensure that the pharaoh is never in any real danger, subduing dangerous wild animals is a way for him to demonstrate his might and courage in public. Archery is also popular with the nobility, and amazing feats – believable or not – have been attributed to pharaohs both past and present. Amenhotep II, for example, is said to have been able to shoot arrows through thick copper ingots while simultaneously driving a chariot.

Everyone enjoys a party in Egypt and there are any number of excuses for throwing one, weddings and birthdays among them. Grand events such as a pharaoh's *sed*-festival, and great religious celebrations, are occasions for the entire land to rejoice. For the wealthy, nothing beats an elaborate banquet complete with an abundance of food, drink and entertainment. If you're sufficiently well connected, try to secure an invitation to such an event. The party will start in the afternoon or early evening and can carry on for hours. When you enter the venue, you will

As an invited guest, expect to be spoiled by attendants during an upscale Egyptian party.

likely be seated by status. Don't be surprised if someone places a sticky cone-shaped mound of fat on your head. As it melts, it will produce a pleasant scent and condition your hair. You might also be presented with a lovely lotus flower for your aromatic enjoyment.

Egypt is not a temperance society: expect large quantities of beer and expensive wine. Some who have attended lavish Egyptian parties report that lotus juice added to wine produces a pleasant euphoria, but their recollections are understandably a little hazy. The Egyptians don't seem to have any real problems with drunkenness, so long as it doesn't result in poor conduct. Drink as much as you like, but avoid fighting and making passes at married women. The food provided will be substantial and may include a whole cooked ox and plenty of fowl, fish and sweet pastries.

As you eat and drink your fill, you will be entertained with music, singing and dancing. The mostly female musicians play an interesting array of instruments: drums and clappers for maintaining

Music and nubile young women are regular features at Egyptian celebrations.

rhythm; harps, lyres and lutes for strumming the melody; and flutes and pipes for the higher notes. Many of the harp players who perform the final songs at parties are elderly men, some of them blind. Expect some lively singing while nearly nude dancing girls entrance the guests. Sometimes love songs are performed, with a young man and a young woman singing the appropriate parts.

Yes, life in Egypt can be hard for the masses but even the most downtrodden peasant experiences occasional moments of joy. A pleasant climate, an abundance of food and a society that values justice and family happiness provides a good quality of life for Kemet's inhabitants – so much so that most Egyptians actually wish for a continuance of such a life in the hereafter.

GODDESSES

The Egyptians have a goddess of beer named Menqet. Hathor, one of the foremost of the goddesses, is also associated with good times as a patroness of music, dancing and even intoxication with such titles as 'mistress of music' and 'lady of drunkenness'.

VII · MIDDLE EGYPT

Sneferu's Pyramids • The Fayyum
Akhetaten: Ghost Town of the Heretic
The Journey Continues

HAVING SEEN THE GREAT CITY of Men-nefer (Memphis) and its impressive cemeteries, some travellers might choose to turn around and head home, satisfied that they've sampled some of the best of the land. But it would be a shame to leave now; Egypt has so much more to offer. Continue your adventure to Waset (Thebes) and you won't be disappointed.

Moving south from Memphis, every province has a capital town that provides some sort of interesting attraction, or at least a place to stay. You can either sail upstream (recommended) or travel on foot, donkey in tow. By boat, expect to take about two weeks to reach Thebes from Memphis, depending on wind conditions and the ambitions of your captains.

SNEFERU'S PYRAMIDS

OFF TO THE WEST ARE THREE pyramids worth visiting if you can. They were built by Sneferu, the first king of the 4th dynasty, and each represents an evolutionary step in the development of Egyptian pyramids after Djoser built his monument at Saqqara. Sneferu began a step pyramid 50 miles south of Saqqara at a site called Djed Sneferu

('Sneferu endures'). At some point well into the construction process, the decision was made to attempt an actual pyramid-shaped structure with four sides, converging to a point and faced with beautiful white limestone. For reasons now long forgotten, the result was apparently unsatisfactory and in the fifteenth year of his reign, Sneferu abandoned this undertaking and moved to another site, 25 miles north, called Dahshur, where he built another pyramid. This one also encountered problems, probably due to a weak building surface: its four sides begin at an impressively steep 55-degree angle and then switch about midway to 44 degrees, giving the pyramid an odd, bent appearance. Apparently seeking perfection, Sneferu began yet another huge pyramid nearby. This time he got it right. His third and final attempt, called 'the shining pyramid', is perfectly proportioned: 345 feet tall with a base length of 722 feet per side. Sneferu's dogged experimentation and pursuit of excellence made possible one of the greatest building achievements of all time: the pyramid of his son, Khufu, which knocked your socks off at Giza.

It took Sneferu three tries to get it right, but eventually he was able to build a competent true pyramid. Attempt No. 2 is pictured above: a curious bent structure that stands at Dahshur.

THE FAYYUM

THE REGION KNOWN AS THE Fayyum also lies to the west, famed for its large lake, the She-resy ('southern lake'). If you choose to make a detour to this area, you'll be able to admire its expansive fields and many estates of the well off. The lake is quite lovely and is connected to the Nile by a very long side branch that parallels the river for many miles. The Fayyum region is considered sacred to the crocodile-god Sobek, so keep your eyes open when travelling near water in case he decides to make a surprise visitation.

Another must-see attraction of the Fayyum is the 'labyrinth' of Amenemhet III (12th dynasty), located near his deteriorating pyramid. The Greek historian Herodotus later reports:

This maze surpasses even the pyramids. It has twelve roofed courts, with doors over against each other:... There are also double sets of chambers, 3,000 altogether, 1,500 above and the same number underground.... The outlets of the chambers and the mazy passages hither and thither through the courts were an unending marvel to us as we passed from court to apartment and from apartment to colonnade, from colonnades again to more chambers and then into yet more courts. Over all of this is a roof, made of stone like the walls and the walls are covered with carven figures, and every court is set round with pillars of white stone most exactly fitted together.

You can decide for yourself whether or not Greeks are too easily impressed, but this enormous and unusual funerary complex is certainly worth seeing – albeit with an experienced guide. Elsewhere in the region, at a site known as Biahmu, you can admire a pair of colossal seated statues of Amenemhet III, fashioned from red granite.

Further upstream on the west bank is the town of Henen-nesut (Herakleopolis). This provincial capital played a central role in the Egyptian civil war about 900 years ago, when the political leaders of Henen-nesut proclaimed themselves the rulers of Egypt and their city its capital, beginning 150 years of strife in the land before Egypt was once again reunited by the leaders of Thebes.

A couple of temples can be found in the vicinity of Henen-nesut and, as seems to be the case almost everywhere you go, if the monuments were not actually initiated by Ramesses II, he has at least enhanced the work of predecessors. Further upstream, you'll pass a temple on a cliff, dedicated to the wild lioness-goddess Pakhet. It was built by the controversial 18th-dynasty female pharaoh Hatshepsut (more about her in Chapter VIII) and contains written boasts of how the queen restored temples that had been neglected since the time of the Hyksos. Ironically Ramesses and his predecessors have now allowed Hatshepsut's temples, including this one, to fall into disrepair in an attempt to erase her from history.

A fair distance further south, you'll come to the town of Khmun (Hermopolis) which can be visited by a canal leading west from the river. Its name means 'city of the eight' which is a reference to the eight primordial gods that are fixtures of some Egyptian creation mythologies. Khmun is a cult centre for the worship of Thoth, the god of wisdom and writing. Some rather large stone images of baboons here (representing Thoth) might be worth a look, assuming you've yet to see such a thing. As usual, Ramesses II has added to the complex and – according to some – has made liberal use of building stones pilfered from the monuments of earlier rulers.

AKHETATEN: GHOST TOWN OF THE HERETIC

APPROXIMATELY 200 MILES SOUTH of Memphis, you'll reach the extraordinary ruins of a once-great city, Akhetaten. Its abandoned avenues, palaces and temples are well worth at least a day's visit. If you've read consistently this far, you will have heard mention of a despised pharaoh by the name of Akhenaten. Who was this character and why is his city now a ghost town?

About 150 years ago, Amenhotep III presided over a 'golden age' when Egypt was especially strong, comfortable and prosperous. Memphis still served as an administrative centre and Thebes was a primary royal residence and the home of the predominant cult of Amun-Ra presided over by a powerful and wealthy priesthood. Amenhotep's successor would have been Thutmose V, but the crown prince died and another son, Amenhotep IV, inherited the throne. This strange fellow initiated a religious revolution, advocating the exclusive worship of a manifestation of the sun known as the 'Aten', essentially the sun-disc with its warmth and powerful rays.

In all of Egyptian history, no one has surpassed the heretic king Akhenaten for sheer oddity.
He is pictured here with his wife, Nefertiti.

Amenhotep IV began building temples to Aten near the cult centre of Amun and during the fifth year of his reign, things took an even more drastic turn. The pharaoh changed his name to Akhenaten ('spirit of the sun-disc') and moved his court many miles north, far away from existing political and religious centres. The new capital, built on undeveloped land on the Nile floodplain, was called Akhetaten ('horizon of the sun-disc'). It was an enormous city, stretching over 7 miles along the east bank of the Nile, bisected by a royal road stretching from north to south. A royal palace and residences were built for Akhenaten and his family. The bureaucrats also all needed their offices and the artisans their workshops. A population of perhaps as many as 50,000 people, both rich and poor, likewise needed accommodations, and elaborate temples were erected for the worship of the Aten.

One should not underestimate the extreme change that Akhenaten attempted to inflict on Egyptian society. He forbade the worship of most of the other gods and conducted a campaign of vandalism against their temples and images, especially those of Amun. Akhenaten's Aten was also quite different from the other Egyptian gods. It could not be depicted in the typical human, animal or hybrid forms used in Egyptian art. Instead, the Aten was

'HYMN TO THE ATEN'

Akhenaten's devotion to the sun-disc is fanatically proclaimed in a poetic 'Hymn to the Aten' which might have been composed by the pharaoh himself. Here is an excerpt:

Splendid you rise in heaven's heartland,
O living Aten, creator of life!
When you have dawned in eastern lightland,
You fill every land with your beauty.
You are beauteous, great, radiant,
High over every land;
Your rays embrace the lands,
To the limits of all that you made.
Being Ra, you reached their limits,
You bend them for the son whom you love;
Though you are far, your rays are on earth,
Though one sees you, your strides are unseen.

represented as the round solar ball from which extend numerous arms, their hands reaching out to warm and caress its human worshippers. As a god supreme, the Aten remained without a consort. Most of the other temples in Egypt centred around a series of chambers leading to a dark room containing a statue of the god, but worship of the Aten took place without a cult image, in large courtyards open to the sun, where the power of the Aten would certainly be felt on clear days.

If anything positive can be said about the whole bizarre Akhenaten-episode, it might be that it encouraged unprecedented innovations in artistic expression, at least temporarily, away from the usual conservative Egyptian standard. Across much of the artistic spectrum, the style became freer if not more realistic. Especially bizarre are the depictions of Akhenaten and the royal family in painting and sculpture. (By this point in your journey, you'll have seen enough traditional Egyptian art to immediately detect any aberrations in style.) With an oddly shaped head and face and a distinctly feminine torso, the 'heretic king' is unmistakable. His wives and children, too, were likewise shown with peculiar physical features, including elongated heads and pot bellies. Although the depictions of nature in Akhenaten's art are vivid and joyous, the king and queen are portrayed as the centre of the world to an extent that even exceeds the narcissistic art commissioned by mainstream pharaohs.

NEFERTITI

Akhenaten's chief wife was named Nefertiti ('the beautiful one has come') and was an active partner with her husband in the Atenist revolution. One way she showed her devotion was to take the second name Neferneferuaten ('beautiful are the beauties of Aten'). Surviving artistic depictions of the royal couple show Nefertiti and Akhenaten in such close cooperation that some suggest that they were co-rulers.

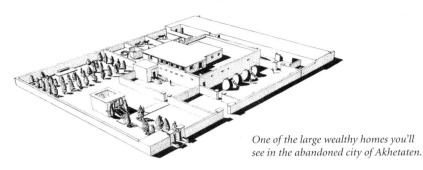

*One of the large wealthy homes you'll
see in the abandoned city of Akhetaten.*

Akhenaten ruled for seventeen years until his death. Many people speculate that he was murdered as there were plenty who suffered under his rule and had reason to want him removed. He built a tomb for himself in a canyon to the east of the city; not surprisingly, it was completely ransacked and there are no traces of his body. Akhenaten was eventually succeeded by a young boy named Tutankhaten ('living image of the sun-disc').

This transition was a perfect opportunity for Egypt's shunned former powers to regain their place. It was not long before Tutankhaten was moved to Thebes and his name was changed to 'Tutankhamun' ('living image of the god Amun'). Following a relatively short ten-year reign, closely controlled by his minders, the eighteen-year-old pharaoh died. (Even the grave robbers no longer remember where Tutankhamun was buried, but maybe one day his tomb will be rediscovered.) He was succeeded by two generals, first Ay and then Horemheb, who made efforts to regain the losses Egypt had sustained during Akhenaten's political upheaval and religious heresy. Horemheb appointed Ramesses I, the present ruler's grandfather, as his successor and a new ruling dynasty began.

The city of Akhetaten was abandoned within a dozen years of the death of Akhenaten and it's a fascinating place to visit. This is one of the few places in Egypt where you can casually wander about and visit a royal palace or the inner courts of a temple – at least what's left of them. With the death of Akhenaten, revenge was taken out on his monuments and you will not find a single one that remains intact. The name of the king was defaced, his images smashed, and his temples dismantled in order to reuse their stone. If people have to refer to something that happened at that time, they generally call it 'the rebellion', and if they absolutely have to mention Akhenaten, it's as 'that criminal'. It's probably not a good idea to discuss the reviled pharaoh with any of your new Egyptian acquaintances: the official policy is that he did not exist.

Begin your exploration of the ruins in the central section of the city, where you will find a large empty palace whose beautifully plastered and painted walls and floors still convey a strong impression of its former splendour. Not far away are the weathered remains of Akhenaten's huge temple, the Per Aten or 'house of Aten'. Within its open courts are over 700 altars and hundreds of brick tables that once served as offering platforms. Piles of bread and other commodities were regularly left here to be displayed and appreciated by the sun-disc shining directly above.

You can then follow the royal road all the way south or north through the city, passing myriad deserted homes and other buildings. You might see a few people living near the river, but there seems little interest in reclaiming this spurned place and the atmosphere is decidedly eerie. To the north of the city centre lies another once-impressive palace; at the southern boundary, try to find what's left of the Maru-Aten ('the viewing of Aten'), a small, pleasant sanctuary that once featured beautiful pools and gardens.

If you're hardy and curious enough, you might be able to convince one of the local inhabitants to take you into the desert to see the elite cemetery. Like the palaces and temples of Akhetaten, it's a rare opportunity to see a genuine royal tomb, albeit one that has been defiled and defaced. Should you find a scrap of linen in the tomb debris, it might even have belonged to the mummy of Akhenaten himself.

As you leave Akhetaten, contemplate the fate of its king and try to imagine

RUMOURS

It is rumoured that many retainers of the 1st-dynasty pharaoh Djer were murdered or committed mass suicide at his death and were interred near their master in his great brick tomb at Abdju. If such was indeed the case, it was a very short-lived (no pun intended!) funerary custom. Egyptian bureaucrats and royal artisans typically serve throughout the reigns of several rulers; their expertise is far too valuable to be sacrificed as a grave offering. Djer's ancient tomb, now essentially a mound, is thought by the present Egyptians to be the site of the actual grave of Osiris.

what might happen to the rest of Egypt's monuments as its empires fall and their physical achievements suffer neglect or wilful destruction.

THE JOURNEY CONTINUES

SOUTH OF AKHETATEN, YOU'LL encounter a few more interesting towns. Zawty (Asyut) features temples to Osiris and a canine deity known as Wepwawet. Further upstream is Ipu (Akhmim), a cult centre for the god Min. Min is usually represented in human form, very obviously ready to perform his role as a fertility deity. You might find such depictions a bit risqué or perhaps amusing but the Egyptians take no special notice; Min is just another character in their complex pantheon. A temple here built by Ramesses II features some especially well-executed colossal statues of the pharaoh himself and his lovely daughter Meritamun. Have a look!

Upstream from Ipu, on the west bank, is one of the most sacred sites in all of Egypt: Abdju (Abydos), a cult centre for Osiris, the god of the dead. The story, in a nutshell, is that Osiris was murdered by his evil brother Seth who cut him up and scattered the pieces. Isis, the devoted wife of the deceased, found them and reassembled her husband, who now rules the hereafter as king of the Netherworld. Egyptians believe that his actual grave is located here. Some of the earliest rulers of Egypt are buried nearby and several temples can be found in the vicinity. Seti's spectacular L-shaped temple features seven sanctuaries to seven gods and was completed by Ramesses II, who recently built another extraordinary temple nearby. These temples are in use and it's likely that you will have to settle for admiring them from the outside. Close to Seti's temple is a special symbolic subterranean tomb for Osiris with great blocks of red granite and a platform surrounded by water.

Because of the strong association with Osiris, untold thousands of pilgrims have come to Abydos from far and wide, and the broken shards from their offering pots are ubiquitous underfoot. Some pilgrims have constructed simple votive chapels or have left little inscribed personal stelae in order to establish their presence near Osiris, even though they'll probably die elsewhere. For similar reasons, at least one 18th-dynasty ruler, Ahmose, built a faux pyramid and associated mortuary structures in the vicinity, although he's actually buried further south in Thebes. Walk around the area and marvel at all the little personal shrines and take note of the rectangular brick superstructures that are the graves of some Egypt's very earliest rulers.

South of Abydos is Iunet (Dendera) with its famous Hathor cult. The nearby towns of Gebtiu (Qift) and Gesa (Qus) are popular departure spots for travellers heading across the eastern desert to the Red Sea. Although you might be tempted to join a caravan or organize one on your own, this sort of excursion is to be discouraged on the grounds that the hardships involved for the tourist will hardly justify the reward. Bandits are known to lurk along the way, and then there's the tricky matter of the return trip.

The great city of Thebes is relatively close now and on its outskirts you'll encounter Madu (Medamoud), a city known for its temples dedicated to Montu, the falcon-headed war-god. Take a look around if you like, but you might consider saving your energy: the greatest city of all is just around the corner. Prepare to be impressed!

VIII · WELCOME TO THEBES!

The City of Thebes • East Bank Attractions
The Female Pharaoh • The Empire Builder
Luxor Temple • Festivals • West Bank Attractions
Some Monuments of the Sun King
The Commemorations Continue • Tombs of Nobles and Kings

IT'S A LONG JOURNEY TO WASET (Thebes) from Pi-Ramesses or Mennefer (Memphis) but for many it's the ultimate destination on a tour of Egypt. There, on both sides of the Nile, you will find extraordinary examples of Egypt's power, the fruits of the empire over many generations. It was the leadership and people of Thebes that settled the

Egyptian civil war many years ago and it was the Thebans who led the drive to oust the foreign Hyksos. In the aftermath, the city served as a home to many powerful rulers, each of whom left their mark in history and in the landmarks of the region. We'll meet a few of these pharaohs as we explore this most remarkable of ancient cities.

With truly spectacular temples on both banks of the Nile, the city of Thebes is a wonder to behold.

As your boat approaches Thebes, there will be no doubt that you've arrived at a city of true wealth and grandeur. The flashing of soaring gold-tipped obelisks reflecting the sun and the convergence of river traffic will tip you off that you are near. Soon the majestic towering walls of temples will appear on the east bank, bedecked with pennants waving in the breezes and guarded by colossal statues and rows of recumbent stone sphinxes. And off to the west, mountains fronted by imposing vertical cliffs provide a backdrop for yet more impressive royal monuments.

THE CITY OF THEBES

WASET, THE EGYPTIAN NAME for Thebes, means 'the sceptre', a fitting appellation given its prominence in Egyptian history. Its reputation is so widespread that it is sometimes simply called 'the city'. Egyptian poets have sung its praises:

Stronger is Thebes than any other city,
She has given the land one master by
her victories.
She who took the bow and grasped
the arrow,
None can fight near her, through
the greatness of her power.
Thebes is the model for every city…

People have lived in the area for thousands of years, and during the time of the pyramids, Thebes wasn't considered of particular importance; it was known mostly as a provincial capital whose local god was Amun. The city rose to prominence during the civil war when a local dynasty expanded its power to the north and south. One of these local rulers, Montuhotep II, was responsible for reuniting Egypt and inspiring a political and cultural renaissance that was fully realized under the rule of the ensuing 12th dynasty, another Theban family. Although these new Theban pharaohs moved their capital north towards the edge of the Fayyum, south of Memphis, the favoured deity of Thebes, Amun, was gradually becoming the state god of the entire land.

EAST BANK ATTRACTIONS

CROWDED, NOISY AND SMELLY streets can be found in any population centre in the land, but that's not what you're here to see. Thebes's untidy urban sprawl surrounds some of the greatest monuments in Egypt. Featured on the east bank of the river are two of the largest religious structures ever constructed by anyone, anywhere, and they remain in active use while continually expanding.

On the north end of Thebes, one finds the great Karnak temple, whose Egyptian name, Ipet-sut, means 'the most select of places'. This mammoth complex is the great national temple dedicated to the state god, Amun. If you approach the temple by water, you will enter via a small harbour that serves as the departure point for ceremonies involving the transport of the god's statue. If you look directly to the east from the harbour you'll have an incredible view of the great temple itself, and its processional avenue lined on both sides with ram-headed sphinxes representing Amun. At the end of the avenue you'll see an immense pylon, gleaming brilliant white and decorated in vivid hues, with colourful flags fluttering from its sides and its entrance portal flanked by two striding statues of Ramesses II. This is probably as far as you, the tourist, will be allowed to proceed, but circling the perimeter of this huge compound should give you a good sense of its beauty and impressive scale.

Karnak temple is by no means the work of a single industrious pharaoh; it has been expanded, if not revised, by nearly every ruler of the last and present dynasty and – majestic as it already is – it remains a work in progress. It started with a relatively small Amun temple established by the Theban rulers who unified Egypt after the civil war about 750 years ago, but the truly grandiose development didn't begin until the 18th dynasty. Since then the temple has grown along its east–west axis, with another portion of it extending south.

Just beyond the great pylon of Ramesses II – if you were allowed to pass – you would proceed immediately into an incredible pillared hall with 134 giant stone columns, some reaching 72 feet in height; their tops carved to resemble bundles of papyrus. Like the rest of the temple, the columns and walls are bril-

A PYLON

A pylon is a gate which, in the case of many Egyptian temples, takes the form of two tall, broad, slightly sloping towers flanking a gate or entrance. Imposing and fortress-like, some are dozens of feet in height and all are designed to impress, especially if their outer surfaces are incised with scenes of military victories. Many pylons have stairs in their interiors that allow access to their roofs.

liantly coloured as part of a decorative scheme conceived under Seti and completed by his son Ramesses. The magnificent hall is illuminated by small rectangular windows close to the roof that let in just the right amount of light to enhance the drama of the interior.

Continuing through this section one will encounter a series of three pylons separated by courtyards, the first built by Amenhotep III, followed by another two constructed by the early 18th-dynasty pharaoh Thutmose I. Hidden between these Thutmose pylons are two of the greatest examples of stoneworking ever accomplished in Egypt: a pair of enormous obelisks commissioned by the controversial female ruler Hatshepsut, 97 feet high and tipped with shining gold. These red-granite monoliths were quarried in Sunu (Aswan) in single pieces, then smoothed and incised with

A colonnaded court in the immense Karnak temple. Don't expect to be allowed inside.

hieroglyphs before being shipped downstream to Thebes. Given that each obelisk weighs more than 320 tons, it is a testament to the skill and ingenuity of Egyptian engineers that they were transported and erected without incident. Sadly, their beautiful inscriptions have now been obscured in an attempt to nullify Hatshepsut's existence.

THE FEMALE PHARAOH

HATSHEPSUT WAS ONE OF THE most extraordinary individuals in the lengthy pageant of Egypt's royal history. Her story begins with the pharaoh Thutmose I, who had a son, also named Thutmose, and a daughter, Hatshepsut, by another wife. The half-brother and sister married, and successfully on the death of their father, Thutmose II became pharaoh for a short reign of only about a dozen years. The male heir to the throne was his son, Thutmose (III), whose mother was not Hatshepsut, but one of Thutmose II's secondary wives. (Yes, the genealogy of these royal families can be quite complicated, but stick with it, the good part is coming!)

At the time of his father's death, Thutmose III was only a small child and certainly incapable of carrying out the formidable responsibilities of the ruler of Egypt. Hatshepsut stepped forward to 'assist' him. Although she was technically sharing the power of the throne with her stepson, Hatshepsut gradually took on more and more of the kingly titles and duties and was serving as the *de facto*

pharaoh. By year seven of the 'co-regency', the charade was over: Hatshepsut took on the full royal titles and even portrayed herself in the male regalia of kingship – sporting the royal false beard and decreasing her bust size in her royal images – while continuing a propaganda campaign to legitimize herself. This, of course, was problematic. Aside from the fact that Hatshepsut had usurped the throne from its rightful heir, the role of ruler of Egypt was with few exceptions an exclusively male prerogative.

Hatshepsut's reign was nonetheless quite successful and marked by some truly incredible building projects, most notably in the Theban area. She also launched expeditions to far-off lands, sponsoring a rare and bold journey south down the Red Sea coast to the exotic land of Punt, which you will see

SENENMUT

For much of her reign, Hatshepsut was served by a commoner by the name of Senenmut. He acquired dozens of official titles and possessed a degree of power unparalleled for a royal bureaucrat, particularly one of low birth. His duties included tutoring Hatshepsut's daughter Neferure. Rumours, of course, were rampant that he was the secret lover of the widowed queen who ruled without a consort.

Back at Karnak, continuing beyond the Hatshepsut obelisks and the Thutmose I pylons, you would pass yet another pylon, built by Thutmose III, and a courtyard that finally leads to the sanctuary housing the temple's sacred image of Amun. A portable wooden boat rests nearby for transporting the statue during festivals. Beyond the shrine is a *sed*-festival hall of Thutmose III, its inscribed walls celebrating his many worthy achievements.

depicted in vivid detail when you visit her memorial temple on the Theban west bank. After a remarkable twenty-year reign, Hatshepsut died from poor health – some say from complications following dental work. Her stepson Thutmose III finally inherited the sole dominion of the throne, immediately beginning the expansion of Egyptian power and influence that continues to this day.

THE EMPIRE BUILDER

SPEAKING OF THUTMOSE III, HE, too, is certainly worthy of a few comments. Hatshepsut's stepson and successor neutralized Egypt's regional rivals in western Asia and far south into Nubia. Truth be told – though probably best not repeated aloud – not even Ramesses II has brought Egypt's power to such far reaches as did Thutmose III during his fifty-four-year reign (if you include

TEMPLES

A hymn to Amun-ra poetically
describes the city of Thebes and the Karnak temple as follows:

'*How mighty she is,*' they said about her,
'*in her Name of Waset, Dominion, the City which shall be!*'
Prosperous in her name of Wadjet, Protecting One;
divine Eye in the Sun-disc before the face of her Lord.
Shining in glory, guiding from her high throne
in her name of Ipet-sut – one without equal.

his 'co-regency' with his step-mother). He was a great builder and you'll see his architectural legacy prominently displayed in Thebes and elsewhere. Later in his life, Thutmose organized a campaign to destroy the royal images of Hatshepsut. It's possible that this state-sponsored vandalism wasn't personal, but was conducted only in order to protect Thutmose's succession, eliminating any precedence for female kingship. In any event, Hatshepsut's name was excised from many monuments and you will not find her recorded on any of the official lists of kings. Still, she left some amazing and thus far indelible marks on Egypt that even Thutmose couldn't erase from the landscape.

Behind the eastern wall of the Amun temple compound are shrines where the common people can appeal to the gods for intercession. There is, for example, a wall inscribed with the image of ears in which devotees can seek advice or otherwise share their concerns with the god Amun himself. Don't be surprised if the mysterious voice that answers from behind the wall sounds suspiciously human. Nearby is what's left of Akhenaten's temple to the Aten, defiantly built in Amun's own backyard. Its dismantled blocks have reportedly been used as building fill for some of the nearby pylons.

In the south-east corner of the Amun temple compound is an artificial sacred lake where the temple priests purify themselves in waters that symbolize the primal seas in Egyptian creation mythol-ogy. The geese that swim in the lake are considered sacred to Amun.

There are other significant temples in the immediate vicinity, including those dedicated to the Theban war god, Montu, and the two other members of the local divine triad, Mut and Khonsu. Mut's temple is approached by an avenue of sphinxes and the complex contains hundreds of statues of the ferocious lion-goddess Sekhmet, who is regarded as an aspect of Mut.

LUXOR TEMPLE

THE SIZE AND SPLENDOUR OF Karnak are certainly overwhelming but the lavish architectural tributes to Egypt's rulers and the god Amun aren't over yet. From Karnak, you can follow another processional way lined with ram-headed sphinxes south for about a mile to another spectacular temple complex known as Ipet Reset ('the Southern Sanctuary') or Luxor temple. The processional way is not in continual ceremonial use, so it may be possible to stroll between the two temples if you go about in a determined and respectful manner, or better yet, accompany a willing priest who is making the short journey.

Luxor temple is designed as a palace for the great god Amun, and incorporates shrines for Mut and Khonsu as well. During the annual Opet festival, the statues of the divine family leave their shrines at Karnak and travel upstream to visit their counterparts at Luxor temple. Much of the temple's

ABOVE: A long avenue lined with sphinxes connects the Karnak and Luxor temples.

construction is attributed to Amenhotep III. Its original structure is the great columned court, which was subsequently expanded outwards. Ramesses II built the great entrance pylon in which stand two obelisks and colossal statues of the pharaoh himself. Should these monuments fail to convince you sufficiently of Ramesses' greatness, the pylon is also decorated with scenes of his heroic feats at the battle of Kadesh, a common motif around town.

BELOW: Flanked by pylons, obelisks and colossal statues, the entrance to Luxor Temple will not fail to impress.

FESTIVALS

MORE LOCAL AND NATIONAL religious festivals take place at Thebes than anywhere else in Egypt. Some are quite joyful while others retain a sombre mood. For average Egyptians, these festivals are the only time they will actually have an opportunity to see the sacred cult images of the gods. The statues are carried about on small wooden boats borne on the shoulders of *wab*-priests as they pay visits to other divine images or sacred sites. Here are a few of the most prominent festivals:

WEP-RENPET is New Year's Day, celebrated on the first day of the civil calendar, around 20 July. There's no reason for you not to join in the general festivities.

THE WAG FESTIVAL is observed about seventeen days after New Year's and commemorates the dead. Unless you know a dead Egyptian, you might want to sit this one out.

THE OPET FESTIVAL takes place in Thebes over twenty-seven days during the second month and is perhaps the most glorious festival in all of Egypt. It can last over three weeks and is well worth attending. During Opet, the image of the god Amun takes a short trip south from Karnak temple to visit Luxor temple. With great pageantry, the enshrined image is carried on the shoulders of priests to the river where it is loaded onto a magnificent gilded ship worthy of a divine passenger. The banks of the river will be packed with noisy and colourful onlookers eager to glimpse the spectacle as the boat is slowly pulled upstream to its destination.

THE SOKAR FESTIVAL, named after a funerary deity, takes place at the end of the fourth month, at the usual culmination of the annual Nile inundation. At this time the death of Osiris is commemorated, followed a few days later by the Nehebkau festival which celebrates his rebirth. Needless to say, the latter celebration is more upbeat.

THE FESTIVAL OF MIN is an agricultural celebration that takes place during

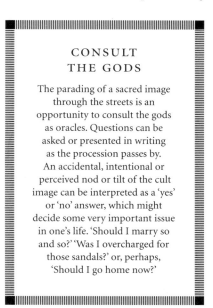

CONSULT THE GODS

The parading of a sacred image through the streets is an opportunity to consult the gods as oracles. Questions can be asked or presented in writing as the procession passes by. An accidental, intentional or perceived nod or tilt of the cult image can be interpreted as a 'yes' or 'no' answer, which might decide some very important issue in one's life. 'Should I marry so and so?' 'Was I overcharged for those sandals?' or, perhaps, 'Should I go home now?'

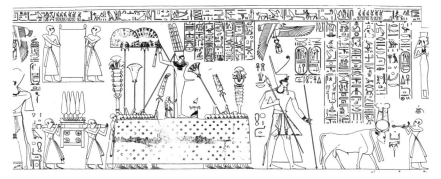

Led by the pharaoh, a statue of the fertility god Min, ready and able, is put on parade during one of Egypt's many religious festivals.

the ninth month to ensure a good harvest. As a fertility god, Min is an appropriate focus for such a festival.

THE VALLEY FEAST occurs in the Theban region during the tenth month. The images of the local triad of gods – Amun, Mut and Khonsu – are brought across the river to visit the funerary temples on the opposite bank, while families visit the graves of their loved ones.

THE SED-FESTIVAL This jubilee celebration for royal rejuvenation is normally only held after thirty years of a ruler's reign, but this regulation is routinely ignored by some pharaohs – such as Ramesses II – who conduct the festival years in advance or hold additional ones at whim. But consider yourself lucky if you happen to be in Egypt on one of these rare but very significant occasions.

In addition to these major celebrations, almost every temple has its own local festivals. As you travel about in Egypt, make enquiries as to which events are taking place. If you can find a way to blend in with the crowd, there's a chance you'll be able to join in one of the public spectacles or at least catch a glimpse of the action. Perhaps your new Egyptian acquaintances will invite you along.

WEST BANK ATTRACTIONS

IN EGYPTIAN MYTHOLOGY, THE sun sets in the west to descend into the land of the dead. At Thebes and Memphis, you will find the tombs and other burial monuments of the elite on the western side of the river. Looking from the east bank, you can admire the natural beauty of the golden cliffs of the Theban mountains under which both pharaohs and ordinary mortals are interred. Here, too, are extraordinary memorial temples, serviced by priests, designed to honour the rulers of Egypt in perpetuity. The royal burials themselves are hidden in a secret cemetery in the arid mountains.

SOME MONUMENTS OF THE SUN KING

TAKE A FERRY ACROSS THE RIVER to the western side and head directly towards the cliffs to visit the greatest memorial park south of Memphis. After just a couple of miles on foot or donkey, you'll arrive at the cemetery via an enormous monument to the late Amenhotep III, its entrance flanked by a matched pair of colossal statues of the pharaoh, a fitting tribute to the glories of his reign.

Amenhotep III was the great-grandson of Thutmose III and inherited the throne when only about twelve years old. For the next thirty-eight years he ruled Egypt during a time of unprecedented power, wealth and stability. Sometimes referred to as 'The Dazzling Sun', he was a great builder, especially at Thebes, and is second only to Ramesses II for commissioning the most monuments celebrating himself. But why not? He could afford it.

His beloved chief wife, Tiye, was closely involved in matters of state like few other queens and the two of them formed the ideal political couple. This 'golden age' ended after the king's death. He was succeeded by his decidedly odd son Amenhotep IV (also called Akhenaten) who, as we have seen (Chapter VII), abandoned Thebes to pursue his curious religious cult to the sun-disc.

Interestingly, Amenhotep III built a splendid palace for himself within

Enormous seated statues flank the entrance to Amenhotep III's memorial temple on the Theban west bank.

AMENHOTEP, SON OF HAPU

One of the most experienced and admired administrators in Egypt's history was a man named Amenhotep, son of Hapu. Born during the reign of Thutmose III in a small Delta town, he was trained as a religious scribe. His reputation for competence grew and in his fifties, he was first appointed as the royal scribe to Amenhotep III and then quickly promoted to Overseer of Works, in charge of the pharaoh's grandiose building projects. This brilliant organizer and architect lived for over eighty years, and his reputation still endures. Royally commissioned statues of him in a scribal pose can be found at Thebes, and in a memorial temple on the west bank. You'll recognize him as the figure seated with crossed legs, stretching his skirt to form a stiff writing desk. In future centuries, he will be deified and worshipped for his skill, like Imhotep of Memphis. Even now you might see his statues being used as intermediaries to the gods.

walking distance of his memorial temple. Called 'the house of rejoicing', this royal residence was beautifully decorated with painted murals on its plastered walls, and even incorporated a small temple to Amun-Ra. A canal leading from the Nile reaches the complex and feeds into a large artificial lake. The palace is still functional and available for the pharaoh when he visits Thebes, but it's not available for you, alas.

THE COMMEMORATIONS CONTINUE

JUST NORTH OF AMENHOTEP III'S memorial temple is that of the present ruler, Ramesses II. As one might expect, his temple is well underway and is intended to be even greater than those of its predecessors. Its colourfully decorated columns and walls pay ostenta-

tious tribute to Ramesses, and its courts house one of the largest statues ever sculpted in Egypt, a depiction of Ramesses seated on a throne, which is 66 feet tall and weighs in excess of 1,000 tons. Most of the other pharaohs have their memorial temples in the vicinity, including Ramesses' father, Seti, whose surprisingly modest and dignified monument is located not far to the north.

You'll notice that Ramesses' temple is surrounded on several sides by a vast network of low mud-brick structures. Some of these buildings provide accommodation for priests and other staff. Others, more importantly, are warehouses where the wealth that pays for the construction of such royal monuments is stored – everything from exotic imported goods to tons of grain and other vital domestic commodities.

The trend for establishing royal memorial temples in Thebes was actually begun by Montuhotep II, the 11th-dynasty king who reunited Egypt after its ugly civil war. Walking a little north from Ramesses' monument and then west towards the mountains, you'll see his huge terraced temple set directly beneath the cliffs, its approach lined with statues and its courtyard landscaped to resemble a garden. Unlike the temples of later rulers in the vicinity, Montuhotep is actually buried inside it. You'll probably be able to at least stroll through the courtyard. Like many of the old monuments of the Memphis necropolis up north, Montuhotep's burial is not particularly well maintained – or heavily policed by priests, which is to your advantage as a visitor.

Directly adjacent to Montuhotep's monument is the truly astounding memorial temple of Hatshepsut, surely one of the most beautiful architectural achievements in all of Egypt. Given the name Djeser-djeseru ('Holy of Holies'), it features a vast courtyard leading to colonnaded terraces connected by broad ramps. As the memory of Hatshepsut

DIVINE DESCENT

Several temples, including sections of the Southern Sanctuary built by Amenhotep III and a portion of Hatshepsut's memorial monument, feature decorations illustrating the ruler's conception and birth. Especially in the case of Hatshepsut, such art proclaims the legitimacy of royal divinity. The pharaoh's mother is shown being impregnated by Amun and then, under the supervision of Hathor, giving birth to offspring of divine descent.

has been much officially expunged from the record, her glorious temple is ignored and much of its statuary has been shattered and thrown into a pit. Visitors, therefore, should be able to stroll unobtrusively up the broad ramp and view the exquisite reliefs on the walls of the terraces. There you'll find a marvellous record of Her Majesty's impressive accomplishments, including the

A relief carving in Hatshepsut's temple depicts members of the expedition she sponsored to the land of Punt, who return bearing live trees.

expeditions she sponsored to the land of Punt to retrieve unusual plants, animals and exotic goods, and the moving of her giant obelisks.

The Theban mountains are sacred to the goddess Hathor and a chapel to her is also found here, as is a temple of Thutmose III.

TOMBS OF NOBLES AND KINGS

STRETCHING ALONG THE HILL-sides beneath the Theban cliffs are the tombs of the rulers of Thebes during the time of the Hyksos, along with more recent tombs of the nobility. Hundreds of tomb chapels can be found here; you should be able to visit some of them if you dress like an Egyptian and don't say too much. They vary considerably in size and many have their own little court-yards. Some are entered via doorways that resemble little corniced pylons, which lead into one or more chambers with plastered and decorated walls. The paintings typically depict offerings being presented to the deceased, scenes of an imagined good life in the hereafter and autobiographical inscriptions proclaim-ing the excellent virtues of the tomb owner or recalling important events in his life. Don't worry about encountering any mummies; they're buried in shafts and chambers well below. As you wander about, you might witness some tombs under construction: carvers hewing chambers in the limestone bedrock, builders constructing mud-brick court-

yards and chapel superstructures, or artists decorating the walls. When plas-tered and painted white, it's amazing how good mud-brick can look.

Although the guardians of the Theban cemeteries probably won't officially admit it, the tombs of the pharaohs of the last and present dynasties lie just on the other side of the cliffs in a pair of 'secret' valleys ('the Valley of the Kings'), known to insiders as 'The Great Place'. After the dismal failure of the old pyramids in protecting their owners, a new, more easily protected hidden necropolis was initiated by Thutmose I and utilized by Egypt's rulers from then on (with the exception of the renegade Akhenaten). The new cemetery was dra-matically situated, with a pyramid-shaped mountain serving as a backdrop, perhaps symbolically representing a pyramid superstructure for all of the regal tombs below. Framed by limestone cliffs whose colours change with the daily passage of the sun, it's a peaceful venue for god-kings to spend eternity.

The royal tombs themselves are said to be tunnelled directly into the limestone bedrock and decorated with esoteric Egyptian funerary texts to guide the king through the Netherworld. The tombs can take years to build and a pharaoh can only hope that his is finished when the time comes. A staggering array of expensive grave goods – including gilded coffins, furniture and even chariots, along with fine clothing and exquisite jewelry – are interred with the pharaoh's mummy. However, it is rumoured that the sealed doors of a few of these tombs have already been breached by robbers. Despite these isolated lapses in security, the valley is well guarded by Medjay warriors and although it's the worst-kept secret in Egypt you'd be foolish to ask about it. Don't even try to visit this place.

Near to the royal cemetery is an isolated village of artisans whose job it is to carve and decorate the royal tombs. The village is supported by the state and supplied with everything needed to sustain its inhabitants in this arid location against the cliffs, where food and even water have to be brought in. Trails lead over the mountains from the village to the cemetery and rumours abound that one the current projects is a massive tomb designed to hold the collective burials of the many sons of Ramesses II. When not constructing tombs of pharaohs, some of the village workers use their talents to build their own final

resting places on the slopes within the town boundaries. You might attempt to visit the village, but it's kept in relative isolation for a reason and its entrances and exits are guarded. Show up with some jugs of wine and a friendly attitude, though, and perhaps doors (and mouths) will open.

Just south of the workmen's village is another royal cemetery you can't visit. Known as the 'Place of Beauties', it serves primarily as a burial place for the wives and relatives of the ruler, including the present pharaoh's beloved wife Nefertari. Her tomb is said to be enormous, with the most beautifully decorated walls of any in Egypt. It's too bad that some of the most brilliant creations of Egypt's finest artists and artisans are locked away to serve the needs of the dead. Perhaps in the future, millennia from now, these treasures will be revealed to delight and inform the living.

IX · SITES SOUTH

Upstream of Thebes · Sunu and Abu · Nubia
Visiting Nubia · A Giant Surprise · Souvenirs
Going Home

FOR SOME TRAVELLERS, THEBES might be a good place to turn around. By this point, you may have had your fill of temples, palaces, funerary monuments, statues of Ramesses and occasional verbal abuse. After visiting places such as Karnak, it might be hard to believe that there's anything more to see in Egypt. Not necessarily. Kemet continues for another 100 miles or so to its natural southern boundary at the Nile's first cataract near the town of Sunu (Aswan). Egypt's influence doesn't stop at the border, but continues a good distance south into Nubia. Before finally packing up and heading home laden with souvenirs and memories, we'll look at some of the sites south of Thebes.

UPSTREAM OF THEBES

JUST ABOUT 7½ MILES SOUTH OF Thebes we find Iuny (Armant) on the river's west bank. The town is another centre for the worship of the war god Montu, as is yet another settlement found a few miles further south on the east bank, Djerty (Tod). This heavy glorification of Montu in the greater Theban region is understandable, given the constant military activity in this area over centuries of Egyptian empire-building. At Iuny, Montu is joined by not one, but two consorts – Iunit and Tjenenyet – multiple wives befitting a god of such power. Continuing upstream, you'll pass through Seni (Esna) where the god Khnum is likewise worshipped along with two consorts, Nebtu and Mehit, and an offspring by the name of Heka ('magic').

Moving on, eventually you'll arrive at two very interesting places, Nekhen (Hierakonpolis) and Nekheb (El-Kab) situated on opposite sides of the river. Nekhen, on the west bank, was an extremely important place at one time, serving as the primary seat of power in Upper Egypt during the formative years of Egyptian civilization. It was probably here that the present conception of Egyptian kingship developed: with Horus as the local god, it's no wonder that the future ruler of the Two Lands would be portrayed as the living manifestation of this deity. There's still a Horus temple in Nekhen; in fact, we're now in an area that can be regarded as Upper Egypt's 'Horus country'. Little else of this once great and influential place is left to visit, as its power was surpassed by Memphis and Thebes over 1,000 years ago.

On the east side of the river is the city of Nekheb (El-Kab) where you'll find further traces of the former importance of this area as an early Upper Egyptian political centre. The local goddess is Nekhbet, the vulture, who continues to serve as a symbol for Upper Egypt, appearing in titles of the king and as an emblem on the forehead of the royal headdress. As you might expect, there is a great temple to Nekhbet here. There are also a number of interesting tombs belonging to powerful governors and other local officials. Under the 12th dynasty about 600 years ago, the power of local governors persisted in the region after it declined in the rest of Egypt. Many important officers in the anti-Hyksos campaigns hailed from this fiercely independent district.

Further south on the west bank is Djebat (Edfu), an interesting town that shares the regional fixation on Horus. About 40 miles before Aswan, the river narrows considerably at the town of Kheny, whose name means 'place of rowing', as the faster-flowing water and whirlpools make navigating the river more difficult here. There are substantial sandstone quarries here and an interesting chapel cut into the rock by the pharaoh Horemheb, dedicated to seven deities including Horemheb himself.

SUNU AND ABU

FINALLY ONE REACHES SUNU (Aswan) on the Nile's east bank. Sunu means 'the market' in Egyptian, and a well-suited appellation it is. Here is the intersection between the known, generally stable world of the Egyptians and the exotic, somewhat volatile lands

IVORY

The Egyptians highly prize ivory as a beautiful, workable material for use in a variety of special objects. It's primarily derived from the tusks of two animals, the hippo and the elephant. Hippos can be readily found in the Nile but the highly regarded elephant tusks require importation through Nubia. There was once a population of elephants in Syria, but they were hunted to extinction with the help of, among others, pharaohs such as Thutmose III, who bragged about killing 120 of these sturdy creatures. When ivory is unavailable or too expensive, some artisans substitute bone.

to the south. Sunu is a relatively small city, overshadowed by the lively settlement of Abu located immediately adjacent on a large rocky island in the Nile. 'Abu' literally means 'elephant', and also 'ivory', and although no live elephants have been seen here for thousands of years, the name reflects the importance of the ivory trade from southern lands. Abu serves as the provincial capital and celebrates Khnum, his consort Satet and their daughter Anuket as its local gods; there are temples to each in the vicinity. For centuries, both Aswan and Abu have been launching spots for expeditions into foreign territories. The towns are teeming with activity as caravans come and go and boats fill with all manner of cargo being shipped to destinations downstream.

The area around Sunu is also known as the source of the best granite in Egypt. Quarries have been in business here from at least the time of the pyramids and they are still being actively worked. Freeing large granite stones from bedrock with stone pounders wielded by hand is a tough enterprise. While in Aswan, you'll see large barges moored on the river banks to receive the immensely heavy materials needed to satisfy Ramesses' insatiable appetite for building. Tourists with a technical interest might enjoy a trip out to the famous quarries. It's fascinating to watch the skill of the workers as they operate in such dangerous conditions, but stay out of the way or you might be crushed as stones are released and moved. Make sure to see the famous giant obelisk, which was being shaped and prepared for release from the quarry when cracks were found in the granite and the project was abandoned. If it had been completed, it would have been twice the size of the largest obelisk in Egypt.

NUBIA

THE LAND BEYOND EGYPT'S southern border is known as Nubia. Upstream from here, rocks clutter the

DANCING PYGMY

Plants, animal and mineral materials were not the only commodities brought from Nubia. The Egyptian official Harkhuf recorded a story about how he obtained a dancing pygmy from the southern land of 'the Horizon Dwellers'. A letter sent to him from the 6th-dynasty king Pepi II (Neferkare) reads:

Come northward to the court immediately; you shall bring this pygmy with you, which you will bring living, prosperous and healthy from the land of the Horizon Dwellers, to dance before the god, to rejoice and gladden the heart of the king of Upper and Lower Egypt, Neferkare, who lives forever. When he goes down with thee into the vessel, appoint excellent people, who shall be beside him on each side of the vessel; take care lest he fall into the water. When he sleeps at night appoint excellent people, who shall sleep beside him in his tent, inspect ten times a night. My majesty desires to see this pygmy more than the gifts of Sinai and of Punt.

Harkhuf was very well rewarded for his efforts.

The cataracts of the Nile serve as a natural southern boundary for the land of Egypt.

river, producing rapids or 'cataracts' that are nearly impossible to navigate. The cataracts form a natural boundary across the Nile that protects the Egyptians from their many potential enemies living in the south. The area from Aswan upstream to the second cataract is called Lower Nubia, and the area beyond it, Upper Nubia. The region has been known for years as home to peoples such as the Wawat, Yam and Irtjet, Medjay and Nehesiu. Egyptians usually refer to Nubia collectively as 'vile' or 'wretched' Kush, which should give you a clue as to what lies ahead.

Nubia is valuable to the Egyptians primarily for the highly desirable goods that are found there, including ivory, exotic woods, animal pelts, cattle and, of course, gold. The very name 'Nubia' is possibly related to *noob*, the Egyptian word for gold. An Upper Egyptian governor by the name of Harkhuf, serving during the time of the pyramids, described some of the exotic products he retrieved on an expedition into region: 'I descended with 300 donkeys laden with incense, ebony, oil, grain, panther skins, ivory, throwing-sticks and every good product', along with cattle and goats.

Egypt's relations with Kush have fluctuated throughout history; at present, things are relatively peaceful, with mutual trading and a substantial Egyptian occupation. During the time of the Hyksos, however, the Kushites took advantage of Egypt's military weakness and advanced to its southern borders.

During the same period, one of the Theban rulers, Kamose, made incursions against the Kushites; there are a number of Egyptian forts and some settlements dating from this era in both Lower and Upper Nubia.

The capital of the Kushite kingdom is a city called Kerma, which lies upstream of the third cataract, about 420 miles south of Sunu. It was conquered by some of the more aggressive pharaohs of the 18th dynasty and the Egyptians still have the place more or less under control. Nubia in general is administered by the viceroy of Kush, who is appointed by the pharaoh and also bears the title 'Chief of Southern Foreign Lands'. This powerful official is served by his own bureaucracy, assisted by Nubian collaborators, some of whom are first sent off to Egypt for cultural indoctrination.

VISITING NUBIA

TRUTHFULLY, VENTURING BEYOND Sunu and Abu is not recommended. The caravan routes that bypass the cataracts are generally arduous. The people you will likely encounter, including soldiers, traders and gold miners, have no experience with 'tourists' and probably won't know what to do with you. Furthermore, as a foreigner, you will have to run the gauntlet of the many Egyptian forts found along the way and eventually go through the hassle of trying to re-enter Egypt at the southern border. Unlike your original entry into Kemet from the north, you can't expect

any professional translators at the southern border who will understand anything other than Egyptian or Nubian, and the soldiers will be suspicious of you, as they rarely see tourists entering from the south.

Should you choose to sojourn south, however, there are a few interesting things to see: some temples and shrines, a few active settlements and a good number of forts manned by Egyptians and Medjay. Join a caravan (which might require that you supply your own donkey), or hitch a ride on a boat to transport you on the long stretch of river between the first and second cataracts. It is not advised that you travel past the well-defended second cataract, but you will nonetheless be very satisfied with making your turnaround at Ramesses' giant monuments at Meha, about 200 miles south of Sunu.

Just a few dozen miles south of Sunu you'll pass the first of seven temples built by Ramesses II in Nubia, all on the west bank on the Nile; yet another lies about 20 miles beyond. Continuing about another 60 miles you'll reach Baki, a major fort on the east bank, where you can find supplies, but very little sympathy. Twenty-five miles beyond are some very interesting temples built by Amenhotep III for Amun and Ramesses II for Ra-Harakhty and Amun-Ra, the latter complete with a sphinx-lined approach and a pylon entrance. When you reach Miam (Aniba), the provincial administration centre for Lower Nubia, your 'homesickness' will be satisfied by the

Carved into the face of a sandstone mountain in Nubia, Ramesses' beautiful temple to his now deceased queen Nefertari is an architectural masterpiece.

presence of Egyptian bureaucrats and soldiers. Have a rest, if so desired, and move on. The biggest Nubian attraction awaits you just upstream. Approach it by boat; you can't miss it.

A GIANT SURPRISE

IF THERE IS ANY TRULY GREAT reward in making the harrowing journey into Nubia, it's a visit to the area known as Meha, north of the second cataract, where you'll find one of the most spectacular of all Egyptian monuments. Along the Nile's west bank, Ramesses has built two enormous temples, carved into the sandstone cliffs, whose size and beauty are difficult to comprehend given the remote location. They obviously

weren't built to impress the relatively few Egyptians who pass by. Instead, by laying permanent claim to the landscape, they dramatically demonstrate to the Nubians the imperial might of Egypt and the power of Ramesses himself.

The larger of the two temples is fronted by four colossal seated statues of Ramesses, each reaching a height of 67 feet. One feels dwarfed even standing next to one of their toes! A huge earthquake, perhaps twenty-five years ago, toppled the head off the southernmost statue and severely damaged the temple's interior. Extensive repairs were made, although Ramesses' head still lies shattered at his feet.

The temple's façade resembles a pylon and a frieze of baboons stretches across the upper face of the carved cliff, greeting the sun. Above the doorway is a giant striding image of the falcon-headed deity Ra-Harakhty, complete with a sun-disc atop his head. If you look carefully at the carving, you'll see that Ra-Harakhty and the hieroglyphic symbols he is holding in his hands – *user* ('power') and *maat* ('truth') – cleverly combine to form the hieroglyphs for Ramesses' throne-name: Usermaatre ('the Justice of Ra is Powerful').

Inside, the temple continues deep into the mountainside and a pillared hall near the entrance features huge standing figures depicting Ramesses as Osiris. Colourfully decorated, the interior walls show the pharaoh at his mightiest including, yet again, scenes celebrating his 'victory' at the battle of Kadesh. In the temple's furthest chamber are found four seated statues representing the gods Ptah, Amun-Ra, Ra-Harakhty and, of course, Ramesses himself. Twice a year, to the credit of the engineers who designed this architectural masterpiece so precisely, a beam of light from the rising sun penetrates through the temple's entranceway to illuminate these divine statues.

It's a quiet and beautiful place here, the blue waters of the Nile contrasting spectacularly with the stark desert terrain. Next to Ramesses' great monument, on a smaller but nonetheless very impressive scale, is another temple cut into a sandstone hill, this one dedicated to his beloved wife Nefertari and the goddess Hathor. Six colossal standing statues grace the exterior, four of Ramesses and two of Nefertari, each about 33 feet in height. If you make discreet enquiries, you may be able to find a priest who will give you a quick – though possibly expensive – glance at the temples' interiors. If not, their exterior grandeur and striking natural setting will still leave a lasting impression.

Although Egyptian strongholds and settlements continue south, it is best to turn around here. Time to return to Egypt, if they'll let you back in, and head for home.

SOUVENIRS

WHATEVER YOUR ITINERARY, you will certainly leave Egypt with a head full of memories and many stories that few at home will believe. But that's not necessarily sufficient. The friends and loved ones you left months ago as you ventured off on your improbable journey will be elated that you've returned unscathed, but in the back of their minds they'll be wondering whether you've brought them a little something from that curious place. Here are some suggestions:

TEXTILES Egyptian linen is a local commodity that looks great and will keep you cool during the summer. Rather than appear alien and foolish by wearing Egyptian garb back home, you would probably do best by buying lengths or sheets of the material to be fashioned into something more culturally appropriate and functional. On the other hand, a linen headdress or elaborate Egyptian wig could delight the kids or the neighbours during a party.

PAPER Paper made from the papyrus plant is a genuine product of Kemet. A roll of this material can be purchased for about 2 deben. Ask a local scribe or artist if they'll be willing to inscribe or decorate the paper with something characteristically Egyptian; perhaps a nice Nile scene with a boat. (You might want to check with a second scribe to make sure that the first one didn't write something to the effect of 'the superiority of the Egyptians is obvious everywhere', 'go home, vile foreigner', or 'I went to Egypt and all I brought back was a sheet of this paper'.

AMULETS Amulets come in dozens of varieties with many choices of colours, sizes, materials and meanings. The cheaper ones are made of faïence, a pretty ceramic material that is typically blue or green, but pricier materials such as gold or gemstones are also options. Ask your amulet dealer about the trendy *ankh*, a symbol of life, the *djed*-pillar of stability, the always-popular scarabs, or the protective *udjat*, the 'eye of Horus'. For that special friend with an insect phobia, a well-made fly amulet might assist in warding off the pests – or perhaps even increase fertility.

JEWELRY If you exchanged most of your metal jewelry for commodities during your trip, you might consider some inexpensive bead creations such as necklaces or bracelets. If wealth is no object, beautiful items exquisitely manufactured from precious stones or metals can be purchased or made to order by goldsmiths, and worn home under one's clothing.

DOLLS Those flat paddle-shaped dolls with hair on their 'heads' that are so popular with little Egyptian girls might provide interesting ethnic souvenirs. Non-Egyptian children, however, might be tempted to hit balls with them.

MONKEYS Forget about them. They make good souvenirs only for your enemies.

A WOODEN OR STONE PILLOW These are novelty items for sure, but they're heavy to transport and will likely end up as a doorstops.

GOING HOME

IF YOU HAVEN'T FOUND YOURSELF sentenced to hard labour in a rock quarry or been eaten alive by a crocodile, it will be time to go home. The return journey by boat should be much faster as you'll be travelling north to south downstream rather than sailing against the current. You'll pass familiar places and perhaps even choose to revisit a few of the sites you found most intriguing. Eventually, you'll find yourself back in the Delta, passing by, or through,

Pi-Ramesses and, if proceeding by land, heading for the eastern frontier fort. If you arrived in Egypt with a donkey and then discarded or sold it, it might be time to find a new one to haul back your travelling equipment and all those souvenirs.

You'll find it easier to leave Egypt than it was to get in. The soldiers might rummage through your luggage on some weak pretence and then send you off. Don't expect any sincere goodbyes from the border staff or a sign that says, 'Come back soon!' Sadly, it's likely that the average Egyptian doesn't care that you visited or whether or not you will ever return. If you made a few new friends during your journey, at least you've left a good impression of outsiders that might benefit those who follow in your wake.

Returning to your previous life after your Egyptian odyssey might require a bit of readjustment. You may long for the beer, the food, the festivals and the parties. If you're from a dry region, you'll probably miss the sight of the broad Nile with its green banks broadening into miles of abundant fields. If you hail from a well-developed city, you might find its architecture somewhat lacklustre and uninspired after the endless parade of grandiose Egyptian monuments. You may also miss the constant intellectual stimulation as you struggled to grasp an alien language, culture and spiritual worldview.

For better or for worse, Egypt will leave its mark on you, whether through happy memories, strange dreams or more likely both. Should you be overcome by the desire to return, however, and political conditions are conducive, Egypt will still be there to tolerate your presence grudgingly once again.

THE GIZA PLATEAU

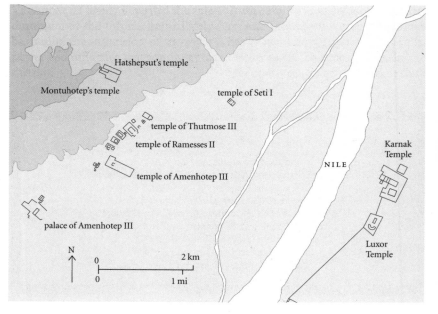

tombs of Khufu's officials

Great Pyramid of Khufu

tombs of Khufu's officials

Khafre's Pyramid

Queens' Pyramids

Great Sphinx

valley temple of Khafre

Menkaure's Pyramid

Queens' Pyramids

valley temple of Menkaure

N

0   200 m
0   600 ft

WASET (THEBES)

Hatshepsut's temple

Montuhotep's temple

temple of Seti I

temple of Thutmose III

temple of Ramesses II

temple of Amenhotep III

NILE

Karnak Temple

palace of Amenhotep III

Luxor Temple

N

0   2 km
0   1 mi

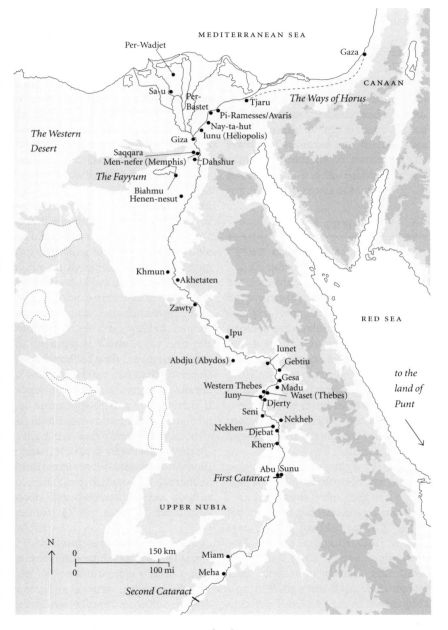

MEDITERRANEAN SEA

Per-Wadjet

Gaza

CANAAN

Sa-u

Per-
Bastet

Tjaru

The Ways of Horus

*The Western
Desert*

Pi-Ramesses/Avaris

Nay-ta-hut

Giza

Iunu (Heliopolis)

Saqqara

Men-nefer (Memphis)

Dahshur

The Fayyum

Biahmu

Henen-nesut

Khmun

Akhetaten

Zawty

RED SEA

Ipu

Iunet

Abdju (Abydos)

Gebtiu

Gesa

*to the
land of
Punt*

Western Thebes

Madu

Iuny

Waset (Thebes)

Djerty

Seni

Nekheb

Nekhen

Djebat

Kheny

Abu Sunu

First Cataract

UPPER NUBIA

N

0   150 km

0   100 mi

Miam

Meha

Second Cataract

USEFUL PHRASES

Your Egyptian vocabulary will grow as you travel, but the carefully chosen phrases below should prove useful as you start your journey down the Nile. Please note that whenever the reigning king is referred to by name or by a title such as 'His Majesty,' it's an important part of Egyptian etiquette to immediately add 'Life! Prosperity! Health! (l.p.h.!) Everyone does it and it's expected that you, too, will show such respect. Good luck!

Hi! My name is _____
Ya! Pay-ee ren _____

Do any of you peasants read hieroglyphs?
In wen wa sekhty yoo-ef rekh shedet medoo-neter er-mi-na?

Does this ship go to Memphis?
In pay menesh nay er Men-nefer?

How many days to Sunu?
Wer herwoo er Sunu?

I need some bread and beer.
Too-ee her atee te henqet.

I love roasted meat and ducks!
Kher mer-ee yoof webed irem apdoo!

I need a clean place to spend the night.
Too-ee her aty wa boo wab yoo yoo-ee er sedjer en-im.

Am I allowed in this place?
In dee-too aq-ee er pay boo?

Life, health and prosperity to all of you!
Imee dee-too en-ten ankh seneb oodja!

You are indeed excellent!
Ya menekh ten!

I am just a foreign fool.
Inek sooga djerdjer.

Egypt is much better than my wretched homeland.
Nefer Kemet er-see er tay-ee khaset kheset.

Are there any hippos, crocodiles or snakes near here?
In wen deboo mesehoo em-ra-poo hefawu aroo?

Truthfully, mummies frighten me.
Too-ee senedj-kooee er-hat sahoo em-maat.

My donkey is ill.
Mer pay-ee aa.

How much (lit. how many deben of copper) for the attractive Bes amulet?
Wer debenoo en hemet er-djebaoo pa sa nefer en Bes?

Does this loincloth make me look fat?
In too-ee kheper-kooee em djeda yoo-ee her wetjes pay daeeoo?

Will His Majesty (l.p.h.!) be attending the festival?
In-yoo Hem-ef (Ankh! Oodja! Seneb!) er eeyt er pa heb?

Look! It's Ramesses (l.p.h.!) the strong bull!
Peter! Ra-mes-soo (Ankh! Oodja! Seneb!) pay, ka nekht!

A statue of Ramesses II (l.p.h.!)? Where?
Wa khentee en Ra-mes-soo (Ankh! Oodja! Seneb!)? Tenoo?

Lovely party!
Heb nefer!

Beer for everyone!
Imee dee-too henqet en boo-neb!

Hey doctor! Is a purge really necessary?
Ya soonoo! In too-ee her aty wat weseshet em-maat?

EGYPTIAN GODS

As an aid to sorting out who's who, here are a few Egypt's more prominent gods and a brief description of each:

Amun Known as the 'hidden-one', Amun converged with Ra to become the king of the gods. His image is usually concealed inside a shrine in the inner sanctums of his temples.

Anubis The patron of embalming and the protector of the cemeteries, Anubis is represented by jackal or depicted in human form with a jackal's head. He's the sort of necessary god that Egyptians are glad to believe in but don't want to spend much time with, at least while they're still alive.

Atum A creator-god, Atum is said to have emerged from a primordial hill of slime and is often associated with the sun.

Geb The god of the earth, Geb is sometimes remembered as a great goose that laid an egg from which the sun was formed. As such, he is also called 'The Great Cackler'.

Hathor A multi-purpose goddess usually depicted as a cow. Hathor is associated with love, fertility, music, intoxication and the night sky. She also has a destructive side to her that can be quite fierce.

Horus The sky-god is often depicted as a falcon or a winged solar disc. The living pharaoh is considered to be Horus, the son of Osiris. When the pharaoh dies, he becomes Osiris, and his son becomes the new living Horus.

Isis Her name means 'throne' and her many roles include associations with love and royal motherhood. In Egyptian mythology she scoured the land looking for pieces of her dead husband, Osiris.

Khonsu The moon-god, the son of Amun-Ra and Mut, is believed to have healing powers.

Maat The goddess of truth and justice is symbolized by a feather or represented in human form with a large feather on her head. Maintaining her stability in the universe is the primary job of the pharaoh.

Min A prominent male fertility deity; you'll know him when you see him. The desert is within his jurisdiction.

Montu The falcon-headed war-god is particularly popular around Thebes.

Mut The consort of Amun-Ra; as such, she is known as the 'Queen of the Gods'.

Neith The goddess of hunting and war is also the patroness of weavers. In some accounts, she is the mother of Sobek, the crocodile god.

Nephthys The protector of the dead is the sister of Isis and the wife of Seth. In mythology she supports her sister, whose husband Seth killed.

Nut Nut is the sky-goddess; the stars can be viewed on her belly each evening. At sunset, she swallows the sun and gives birth to it again in the morning.

Osiris Ruler of the Netherworld and chief judge of the deceased, Osiris is usually depicted as a mummy with green or black skin symbolizing fertility and resurrection.

Ptah The patron of artists and craftsmen and the chief god of Memphis is sometimes also associated with a god of the dead, Sokar. Ptah is usually depicted in human form wearing a blue cap.

Ra The sun-god has many different manifestations, including the falcon-headed Ra-Harakhty.

Seth The epitome of disorder and chaos, Seth was responsible for the first death in the world, that of his brother Osiris. Interestingly, Ramesses II's father, Seti, was named after Seth.

Thoth The god of writing, mathematics and medicine, among other things, also associated with the moon. Thoth is typically depicted as a baboon or an ibis.

AUTHOR'S NOTE

The setting of this book is 1250 B.C. during the fifty-fourth year of the reign of Ramesses II, who ruled Egypt between about 1304 and 1237 B.C. Egypt then was particularly powerful and internationally engaged, making this an extraordinarily interesting time to visit. The majority of texts cited in this work are chronologically appropriate, with the notable exception of those of the Greek historian Herodotus, who toured Egypt c. 450 B.C. and whose writings are still consulted by modern Egyptologists.

I would like to acknowledge the fine Egyptological advice offered by Edmund Meltzer, a superb scholar and a good friend, and Aidan Dodson in the writing of this little book. I would also like to thank Colin Ridler and all the staff at Thames & Hudson who have facilitated this wonderful series of time-travelling tomes.

This book is dedicated to some of my favourite travellers: Sherry Ryan, Patricia Armstrong, Jane Hayes, Dorothy Shelton, Lois Schwartz and Barbara Mertz.

SOURCES OF ILLUSTRATIONS

Art Archive/Bibliothèque des Arts Décoratifs, Paris 83; from Prisse d'Avennes, *Atlas de l'histoire de l'art égyptien*, Paris, 1868-78 9a, 12, 21a, 33, ,38, 68, 98a, 99, 103, 127, 129; Staatliche Museen zu Berlin 105; British Library, London 78; British Museum, London 62; from E. A. Wallis Budge, *Gods of Ancient Egypt*, London, 1904 25, 27; from J.F Champollion, *Monuments de l'Égypte et de la Nubie*, 1835 8; Franz-Marc Frei/Corbis 49; Gianni Dagli Orti/Corbis 52, 53b; Sandro Vannini/Corbis 53a, 54-55; from N. Davies & A. Gardiner, *Ancient Egyptian Paintings*, 1936 31; from N. de Garies Davies, *Mastaba of Ptahhatep and Akhethetep at Saqqareh*, London, 1900 37; from N. de Garies Davies, *Tomb of Nakht*, London, 1917 18; from *Description de l'Égypte*, Paris, 1809-28 2, 36, 42, 47, 56, 73, 75, 98b, 101, 112, 119; from A. Erman, *Life in Ancient Egypt*, London, 1894 9b, 13, 19, 20b, 21b, 40, 61, 66, 67, 82, 85, 98, 109; De Agostini Picture Library/Getty Images 90-91, 96; after H. Gressman, *Altorientalische Bilder zum Alten Testament*, Berlin, 1927 15; after Lepsius, *Denkmaler aus Aegypten*, 1849 121; after P. Newberry, *Beni Hassan*, 29; Metropolitan Museum of Art, New York 20a, 50-51; H.M. Herget/National Geographic Stock 92-93; Robert W. Nicholson/National Geographic Stock 94-95; Musée du Louvre, Paris 89; P.P. Pratt 106

INDEX

Page numbers in *italic* refer to illustrations.

Designed by Liz Rudderham

© 2010 Thames & Hudson Ltd, London

First published in 2010 in paperback in the United States of America by
Thames & Hudson Inc., 500 Fifth Avenue, New York, New York 10110

thamesandhudsonusa.com

Library of Congress Catalog Card Number 2009900128

ISBN 978-0-500-28788-0

Printed and bound in China by Toppan Leefung